REASONS *to* LIVE

REASONS

to

LIVE

An Interactive Guide to Healing
and Overcoming Suicidal Thoughts
and How to Help Others Survive

Juliana J Bruno, a.k.a. Juliana Jay

BOOKS THAT SAVE LIVES

MIAMI

Keep these numbers handy, accessible, and at the ready. Know that you are not alone;
there are people who can help you.

988 Suicide and Crisis Lifeline: 988
Lifeline Chat: 988lifeline.org/chat
Crisis Text Line: Text HOME TO 741741

For permission requests, please contact the publisher at:
Mango Publishing Group
5966 South Dixie Highway, Suite 300
Miami, FL 33143
info@mango.bz

For special orders, quantity sales, course adoptions and corporate sales, please
email the publisher at sales@mango.bz. For trade and wholesale sales, please
contact Ingram Publisher Services at customer.service@ingramcontent.com or
+1.800.509.4887.

Reasons to Live: An Interactive Guide to Healing and Overcoming Suicidal Thoughts
and How to Help Others Survive

Library of Congress Cataloging-in-Publication number: 2024938788
ISBN: (print) 978-1-68481-608-8, (ebook) 978-1-68481-609-5
BISAC category code PSY037000, PSYCHOLOGY / Suicide

To my mother,

Without you, my words would have never found the page.
Thank you for your incredible inner beauty and strength.
My deepest regret is that I did not see all of you until you
were gone.

*"The most beautiful rocks are those
that have weathered the storm."*

—Unknown

TABLE OF CONTENTS

FOREWORD

BY DR. JOHN DUFFY

I know well how a sense of hopelessness can mark a life, an entire family, and a community. I grew up in one of those families. My beloved younger brother Tom took his life years ago, and the shock of that still resonates with me and my family today. This is a big part of what inspired me to become a psychologist. I don't want anyone else to suffer the way Tom did—the way our family has. In fact, the focus of nearly all of my work over the last twenty-five years is on helping struggling teens and tweens, especially boys and young men. We live in such stressful times; I call it the "Age of Anxiety." Tension runs rampant in today's society, and things such as major world events and the constant news cycle can drive enormous worry and feelings of consternation. I'm especially concerned about vulnerable populations such as the youth, LQBTQ+ community, veterans, elders, and others feeling loneliness and isolation. People often find themselves in circumstances that cause deep, dark depression and general feelings of unease, all of which can lead to hopelessness and can often be accompanied by a sense of shame. People can get stuck in such despair, where they feel there is nowhere to turn and that they need to hide from others during a time where companionship and a sense of belonging is vital.

Our society has a long way to go in supporting people's mental health. In the past eight years, the rate of anxiety rose over 30 percent, and, a few months ago, NPR shared an in-depth study of teen girls, a majority of which shared reports of fear and little hope for their futures. In my new book, *Rescuing Our Sons*, and other current research, I find that teen boys and young men are increasingly isolated and further isolating themselves, which can lead to self-harm and violence. Obviously, children are the future of our society, and we cannot allow this to happen. In my work, my books, and my writing, I offer solutions and a call to action to do better by our young people and vulnerable populations. It can be as simple as checking in on a neighbor, staying in touch with a relative, or volunteering at a community center. Just a little bit of time and kindness can go a long way in helping others.

Juliana Bruno's *Reasons to Live* is exactly the book I wish I could've given my younger brother. It is a book I will keep readily available in my office for anyone who finds themselves in that dark place. I am pleased and proud to contribute to Mango Publishing's "Books That Save Lives" imprint. There is no more important work than saving lives and supporting our loved ones and our community.

—Dr. John Duffy, author of *Parenting the New Teen in the Age of Anxiety* and *Rescuing Our Sons*

Prologue

HOW THIS BOOK CAME TO BE

Hello Dear Friends,

This book is not what you think. It isn't about clinical modalities and ideas, although many are mentioned here, nor is it a medical reference guide. This book is about community. It is about you and me and everyone else who is reading this. It is a collective nod of understanding between us. I am not here to tell you how to be or where you went "wrong." I am here to tell you that you are human, and humans hurt. Humans feel with their mind, body, and soul. They feel all there is, all at once. They ache with a pain that has been woven into every part of who they are. They work on change, give up, cry ten thousand tears, and then ten thousand more. They rant, they spew anger bullets at all that stand near, they regret, they are frozen in fear, memories debilitate them, they are broken into a thousand pieces, and each piece is broken into a thousand more. They are lost in the dark woods. They are left without water in a never-ending desert. They are in the badlands of the mind and a drought of the soul. Whatever landscape you find yourself in, look around. You aren't alone. There are more of us out there in the badlands than those beautifully posed on clouds of bliss. We are a community. I see you. I hear you. You matter. You are enough. I love you.

Throughout this book, I will be brutally honest with you, making sure I come to you with the most authentic and brave truth I can possibly bring. I can only offer you what I know, my experiences, and how I emerged from my own darkness.

Before we begin, there are a few truths I will give you as tools along this journey.

- Your emotions are not wrong.

- You are not broken.

- You are already complete, even though it may not feel like it.

- Your inner wisdom knows the path, even if you are overwhelmed and your vision is clouded.

- You are loved.

- You are enough.

- Your feelings are valid.

- Your story is essential, and some of us want to hear it.

- Your voice and your words are the salvation of others.

- You have something to contribute that is beautiful and rare.

Along this journey, people will struggle to hear you or even ignore your words. Know that it isn't you. It is the failure of our society—the failing to love each other deeply enough to be there for one another. We lack the tools, the language, and the compassion to listen to someone screaming in pain. We feel worthless because we can't help. But this thinking is incorrect. We do know how to be there for each other. We may trip or stumble, but each of us has the capacity to support someone in a time of need. It is written in our hearts; we must open to that power, let ourselves remember our connections to one another.

What I outline here is not the only path along this journey. There are many roads you can take and many avenues you can explore. Along with finding a good therapist and working within the healthcare system, many modalities fall within "alternative" or "spiritual" categories. None are right or wrong, but all offer a path. Finding what works for you is crucial. Often, it might be a combination of therapy and alternative modalities. For me, it was important to find belonging and purpose. It was through meditation and a simple conversation with someone capable of deep listening that my healing began. I began to feel the warmth of the sun on my back again—the warmth of healing. You do not need to be fixed, changed, or corrected, but you do need to find your way. Although the responsibility to heal is yours alone, many will support you. You can do this. I believe in you.

Give some thought to what you need. What must you do to find a plausible path to value and purpose for yourself, your life, others, and for what is yet to come? How do you find excitement for it all? What is your path? You have one, but somehow, the stepping stones have been covered up and need to be more visible. Where are they? Be curious and start with a step. Wrong turns are okay; this path isn't a straight shot. Consider healing a labyrinth of choices with only one entrance: your birth. Know that your life is the weaving of everything. It can be wonderful and dark, but most importantly, the safety you seek lies within your labyrinth of self.

This book is not told from the perspective of a therapist or medical doctor, nor will it explain medical models or what you should do and how you should do it. This offering is made by someone who has gone through it; I have been on both sides. This is a person coming to you with compassion. I want you to know that you are here; you are valid, and you will make your way as it works for you. I believe you know the path; this is just a guide to uncovering your way, your stepping stones, and your landscapes.

Although I went to therapy and worked on myself, read many books, and even attended groups and workshops, it was in the community of mindful seekers and alternative folks that I found a reason to live; a reason to be. For you, it might be a deep desire to express yourself creatively or to find people who resonate with the ideas you hold sacred. It might be just playing basketball. Who am I to say, but one thing I do know: you know what you need to heal. You have the strength and bravery to know.

I cannot give you finite observations that will "cure" your thoughts. I do not have all the answers for effectively aiding someone lost in darkness. These powers lie within you, and you already know these things.

I will guide you, but your own openness will give you the answers. As you read this book, find a space to be open to the content and to work with it in a way that resonates with you. If you come here expecting to denounce, judge, and ridicule, you will not be able to hear your own wisdom. Consider vulnerability and openness the doors to your knowing.

You can move forward, and help others to do the same, if you come to the space this book provides with a sense of letting go. Let go of all the recent armor you have collected, defense mechanisms, judgments, and anger you use to guard yourself. These things will not be needed in these pages. They will only hold you back.

Know that I will support you throughout this journey in the best way I know how, with solidarity and truth as I know it. All I ask of you is that you listen deeply, with an open heart.

You must embark on a journey to your true self. Become curious. Like, for example, when you were a child, and the garbage truck came by, or you saw a train going somewhere. Be curious for no other reason than to figure out why. Be curious about yourself. Switch the focus from the incredible pain you feel to the power within. Tap into your inner fabulous self and discover what it has to say. Throughout this book, there will be exercises and thought directions. Try them on, and work with them. Be curious about them.

This book came into being through another manuscript I was writing, in which I was dealing with the death of my mother. My mother had decided to stop fighting her cancer. What followed for me was overwhelming grief and regret sprinkled in with memories, both wonderful and tragic. That was the book I pitched one Saturday morning to the publisher who helped bring this book to life. But she had other ideas, a book on suicide. This occurred after I was asked to "tell a little about myself," and I announced that I had a grassroots suicide awareness organization and that I had worked with nationwide organizations on suicide awareness for a time. She took that information and created a space for this manuscript to emerge.

A few months earlier, I had joined a writing group, where I met some amazing women who were also seeking answers. Some had done the work and reflected on it from a healthy place, and a few of us were in the thick of it. One or two, in particular, were dealing with some deep-rooted grief and sadness. And oh my god, their writing! It is so beautiful, genuine, and sometimes hard to swallow. It was perfect. Jennie, also in the depths of grief, joined about the same time as I did. She and I spent a good four to five months writing about grief, tragedy, loss, sadness, and despair. We often joked that we didn't know how to write much more than long dissertations on grief, regret, and unworthiness. It was amazing how some of these incredible women could take an innocent writing prompt like "bliss" and turn it into a dark, oozing tar that we all felt repelled by, yet attracted to at the same time. Reflecting back, perhaps a few of us were writing ourselves out of our own versions of darkness at that time. Hand in metaphorical hand, we were walking through it, feeling our way out. I cannot tell you how much I appreciated the solidarity of souls in this group as we all grappled with a demon or two. I tell you this because that is an example of finding healing in unusual places. Be open to healing in unexpected places. Healing can be found in a quote on a page, a reflection overheard on the bus, a meme, a joke, a sad story, or a haunting song. Healing is constantly flowing to you in small ways and in big bursts.

Darkness is a place we all find ourselves inhabiting from time to time. We may not plunge into the extremes that lead us to suicidal thoughts, but grief, loss, tragedy, and trauma are a vocabulary we all speak now and again. A good friend once told me that you aren't doing it right if you don't have some dark times. I think there is truth there. Life is not about crispy, perfect moments strung together on the handmade solid gold thread, but rather a menagerie of tangles consisting of human hair, blood stains, and love notes thrown in with wads of chewed gum and precious jewels. It is all beautiful because it is the making of us. It is our soul, as we know it, that is learning how to be human.

Some days, every cell in your body will hurt. Remember the tools from the truths we talked about earlier. You are valid. No matter how you feel, whatever emotions you have, you are valid. You are going to feel this as you are supposed to feel it. It will hurt like a motherfucker, or you may be numb as dense, iced-over, dirty snow. I know. My heart aches for you, but even though I have been there, I do not know your pain. The only person who knows is you.

If anything, this book is a list of tools and information gathered from souls who have approached this subject matter from different angles but still occupy a mutual space of healing. There is no right or wrong way, only your way.

I was lost in the dark woods once and trying desperately to survive, although, I must admit, there were many days when I wondered why survival was important. I have had desperate moments where letting go of my life seemed like my only option, but it wasn't. I read a quote recently on social media that resonated with me—something about how those of us who have faced darkness with courage, love, and acceptance have the potential to experience an unfolding of a much more profound and gratifying life. Finding riches in the darkness gives us something more profound and beyond all that we knew before. I could not agree more. Had I acted on the notion that death was my only answer, I wouldn't be here. Writing this book. Knowing you.

So here I am in this book, telling you what I have learned and how I returned to the place of my deep inner self. Honestly, I had never taken the time to know myself before. I was too wrapped up in the idea of what I was to other people. Who I knew to be me was only a reflection of the expectations of others. I did not know my authentic self. If I can wish for anything for you, it is that you come home to your beautiful and haunting self. That you realize just how incredible life is, how incredible you are, the journey is, the ride, and the infinite potential that lies at your feet. So, dear friend, I offer this flashlight, as it were, the light to get out of this dark space. May we journey forward together toward a place of profound experience, much too incredible to ever leave.

Part I

FOR ALL BODIES

This is an offering of ways to look at human experience and interactions. It outlines a few ways to better understand people around you and to communicate in ways that allow you to be heard. Through these different vantage points, you may learn more about yourself and how you have come to interpret your life, beliefs, emotions, and understandings. There are also many other ways to view our connections to our bodies, thoughts, emotions, beliefs, and actions, as well as connections to cultures, spiritual practices, and modalities. I offer a few here as an invitation to understanding on a deeper level.

1.

PEOPLE IN CONTEXT

"You're missing the context of my thoughts.
Don't misinterpret."

—enlatia, *Pandemiconium: Viral Conspiracy*

People in Context, Thoughts in Context, Understanding Context

I am referring to the people or groups that are interacting within a particular context. For example, perhaps the context is social, historical, cultural, global, or educational in nature. Context is the framework by which people interact. Context affects how a person may perceive or react to things. We are all in context on both macro and micro levels. We may find ourselves in a particular political, cultural, and/or economic context throughout our day, but if we go to a party, we might find ourselves in a micro context of "a party with strangers." At the same time, we carry some deep-rooted context that we consider part of our identity. We also encounter new contexts that we must navigate.

Context can be affected by and may include many things, such as environment, place, nature, and objects. Still, it can also include things that are less tangible, like biases, perceptions, abilities, beliefs, money, constraints, culture, customs, emotions, decisions that have been made, habits, goals, health, income, identity, family beliefs and structure, language, social cues, media, and so on.

The use of context is powerful when making judgments and understanding. It is deeply embedded in our communication, the words we choose, and how we define things around us. It helps us decide how we will act in certain situations. For example, we may act one way at work but another when out with friends. We may use different languages, dress differently, relate to people differently, and so on. We may use context to create self-definitions, such as "I am unhealthy, I am poor, I am uneducated," etc.

The reality we choose to acknowledge is a construct of context. If you had a different context, you might interpret the world in a vastly different way. For example, if you time-traveled to a hundred years in the future, you might recognize certain things, but your context would be from a hundred years earlier. You would be experiencing that time through a lens from the distant past.

Why does this matter to us? Throughout this book, we will be discussing feelings and perceptions. It is important to understand that context is different for everyone and at different times. Understanding context can help you interact effectively and with more care. It can give you insight into the person you are trying to help. It can help you articulate your feelings in a way that makes you feel heard.

Understanding the context of another person allows you to come to them in a place that is in between or be able to meet them where they are. You have a better chance of being heard if you can do this. If you can do this, you can find empathy and compassion. If you cannot meet someone where they are, you will struggle to be understood and heard. Your words may be understandable, but they won't land where you want them to.

Knowing this can help you identify and understand different beliefs, emotions, understandings, patterns, and responses that shape conversations. In short, it helps us improve our communication with others because it is a tool we can use to foster compassion, empathy, understanding, and commonality.

We can even cling to context so tightly that we cannot see other realities, viewpoints, and perspectives. Very strict cultural or religious beliefs can blind us to parts of ourselves and others that are rich and valuable.

Exercise

What are the context frameworks that define your landscape? Can you make a list? How do they relate to your beliefs, emotions, definitions, and actions? When does context change for you? How does that change feel?

Start noticing others and the context frameworks they might be working in. Is it possible to bridge the spaces where you differ to find a meaningful connection?

2.
—

THE INTERSECTIONS BETWEEN OUR INTERNAL LANDSCAPE AND OUR SOCIOPOLITICAL CONDITIONS

"An environment is also an inward reality."

—James Baldwin

The internal landscape takes many forms, depending on the context. For the purposes of this book, I am talking about how we see ourselves through experiences, beliefs, emotions, memories, images, ideas, and internalization of outside beliefs. Your inner landscape is not just your imagination or mind's eye; it is where your spirit and nature reside. It is the terrain of the self. How you see yourself, define yourself, and understand your feelings is through the panoramic view of your life. It is through this view that you determine who you are—in this vast countryside of self, where we often retreat to rejuvenate and restore. We may also go here when we are grappling with outside stimuli. Some of us retreat into our inner landscape when we feel uncomfortable in the outside world. Our inner landscape helps us to define things like what a community is, what a home is, what is safe and what is not, what is positive and what is negative, and so on.

It is common to carry a landscape from memory forward in your mind. You often hear statements like, "The ocean is my church," "My home is actually in the town I grew up in," "My journey is a long road," or "My path is windy." Even the Beatles song "The Long and Winding Road" uses landscape metaphors to describe a feeling.

Nature is such a powerful influence on our overall emotional and mental state. I remember living in the dense part of a major city, where there was nothing but cement and brick. Over time, I became so hungry for the sight of a tree or any type of greenery. I grew up on a ranch, surrounded by trees and pastures, and the memory of green made me feel safe and comforted. What nature is part of your memories, and how does it weave into your emotions, beliefs, and understandings?

Your landscape may have boundaries, hills, edges, and mountains; it may be cold and windy, sunny and dry, lush or desert-like. Visualizing your inner landscape helps you to determine how you feel about things, where you are on your journey, and where you can go. It can be a powerful visualization that can help you find your way or move you forward when you feel stuck. It can be a way to check in with yourself. Closing your eyes and imagining your landscape can help to tell you where you are at any given moment.

Visualization Exercise

Find a comfortable, safe place to settle in for about ten to fifteen minutes. Close your eyes and imagine your mind as a landscape.

Take a moment to look around.

Notice.

What does it look like?
Who is there?
What is the weather like?
How far can you see?
Are there rolling hills or cliffs?

Do this a few times and ask yourself, "Does it change from time to time? If so, how?"

Now that you have looked at your internal landscape, let's look at the sociopolitical factors that also make up your identity. Sociopolitical factors are anything that is a combination of sociological and political factors that influence the actions, beliefs, and understandings of people and groups.

Issues like human rights, sexual harassment and assault, homelessness, healthcare, discrimination, poverty, and immigration are examples of sociopolitical factors. Anything

can be a factor. These factors affect all bodies and groups. For
example, the consequences of poverty can be poor health,
inability to access education, isolation, discrimination, and
limited possibilities. These factors directly affect social justice
and equality. Certain bodies experience profound discrimination
because they identify with a group that has been labeled as
inferior, wrong, bad, predators, villains, criminals, and so on.

It is somewhat easy to connect the dots from sociopolitical factors
to influence on a body, but other consequences might be more
hidden. We can understand the limiting factors and how they may
play into the shaping of beliefs, ideas, identities, and behaviors, but
there are other less evident factors, such as shame, unworthiness,
self-hatred, insecurities, and mental health issues, just to name a
few. Different bodies experience these factors in different ways.

When working with someone, it is essential to consider the factors
that might be affecting them. As you work to identify your internal
landscape, it is important to consider what sociopolitical factors may
have influenced your beliefs, ideas, actions, and understandings.
Even if you did not directly experience a factor personally, some
factors can indirectly affect you. Perhaps your parents have
experienced something that you personally have not, yet their
experiences are shaping your ideas and beliefs. For example, if your
parents or grandparents were immigrants, but you were born in your
current country of residence, then perhaps the sociopolitical factors
they experienced directly are indirectly affecting you.

Make a list of the factors you recognize within your
community or that you have personally experienced.
How have they shaped you and your community? Give
some thought to how they have influenced you and
others. What factors do you see that are influencing your
thoughts, emotions, actions, and beliefs?

3.

IDENTITIES

*"We must educate ourselves about who we are,
what our real identity is."*

—Deepak Chopra

Identities that Carry Power & Privilege

These social identities are often defined by economic status, ethnicity, gender, religion, sexual orientation, and physical representation. These biological and cultural markers alone may afford someone more power and privilege than others. Advantages are given to certain folks who are perceived to be part of certain groups or societies.

These inequitable advantages and distribution of power create exclusion, inequality, and disadvantages for some, while creating disproportionate advantages for others.

The identities associated with power and privilege move the tides of social reactions and treatment of various bodies and groups. In turn, these identities shape an individual's perspectives on others and the world around them. Significantly, these concepts affect how someone moves around the world. For example, an affluent cis white male may navigate the work world differently than someone from a lower-income background who present as a Black trans woman.

These identities influence how we move, our body language, our biases, our thoughts, beliefs, emotions, expression of emotions, our relationship to emotions, our views on mental illness, poverty, health, wellness, and even what we view as necessities in life. Moreover, they affect how we hear what people are saying and how we communicate. Feelings of being misunderstood or devalued can easily become part of someone's identity.

These inequalities are the basis for much of today's social justice work. Social justice is about creating allies and collaboration to promote equality, inclusion, respect, equity, and equal rights for all bodies in all social groups and communities.

Learning how to understand these identities and how to create a safe, understanding, and inclusive space for folks can be lifesaving. Giving folks a space to talk about themselves is as important as learning how to advocate for your needs in a way others can understand.

Identities More Burdened by Marginalization and Oppression

[Important: Related to Who We Might Consider More at Risk for Suicidal Thoughts, Gestures, Behavior]

According to the CDC, suicidal thoughts and behaviors are influenced by conditions a person experiences in their community. This includes work, home, play, or any setting that we inhabit. These conditions are sometimes referred to as social *determinants of health*. They can include, but are not limited to, racism, prejudice, poverty, discrimination, housing insecurities, and barriers to education and/or healthcare. It can be lack of access to transportation, food insecurities, loss, unsafe spaces, fear of being unfairly accused, profiling, violence, rhetoric in the media, and lack of learning opportunities and tools. All these factors create more stress and feelings that can lead to suicidal thoughts or actions down the road.

Moreover, some communities have limited or no access to medical care, therapists, and other modalities of healthcare and healing. Because of these factors and other social conditions, some populations experience more of these issues than the general population. This directly correlates to higher rates of suicide and suicide attempts. The increased rates of various issues in some communities are sometimes referred to as *health disparities*. These populations include but are not limited to veterans, LGBTQIA2S+ people, people living in rural areas, indigenous populations, BIPOC people, people with illness or disabilities, and middle-aged and older folks.

Suicide rates differ by job as well. Your job can also put you at higher risk. Many of these jobs are held by people without access to education or connections for upward mobility.

4.

WELCOMING ALL PARTS OF OURSELVES, OUR INNER AND OUTER SELVES, OUR BODIES, ALL OF IT!

"I surrendered myself to the cages of others' expectations, cultural mandates, and institutional allegiances."

—Glennon Doyle, author of *Untamed: Stop Pleasing, Start Living*

All Parts Are Welcome, Welcoming Our Multiplicity

[Inner and Outer]

Some psychologists refer to the self as having three major components: the outward persona, which is the one you project to the world and others; the experiential self, which is closely tied to memory and how you move through time; and the private self-conscious system, which is your self-concept, beliefs, morals, and values that creates the internal description of who you are. Here, we are talking about the inner you and not concentrating on your body yet.

I remember struggling with this in my teens, feeling like the person I presented to the world was not the person I felt I was inside. I remember feeling that specific memories were so unpleasant that I wanted to wipe them from my being. They felt like tarnished parts of my mind that were rusting and corroding good memories. I was at odds with myself. I think many people feel like this, especially if there is part of their self-conscious system that they feel would not be received well by the outside world. In essence, you feel like you are pretending to feel like someone else. This can become the soil that will grow the seeds of shame and self-hatred.

It is essential to realize that all parts of you are welcome here. All parts. It is crucial to understand that we all have these components of self. We all have an internal landscape and an external garden. We manicure the external maybe a little bit more than the raw and rolling wildlands of our internal self. We all do this. You are not alone. It is essential to recognize this and to realize that sometimes, especially if we are not feeling safe, we may not share some of who we are. This is not inauthentic; it can feel like survival when you feel as though the spaces you live in are not as safe as you need them to be. It's okay; we have all been there.

Then there is your body, the vehicle we use to get around. While we all have relationships with our bodies, these relationships are complicated. As we move through life, our relationships with our bodies change. We develop negative perspectives of our bodies for many reasons. Again, things like sociopolitical factors, context, identities of privilege and power, family beliefs, societal conditioning, media, and so many more factors play a role in the relationship we have with our bodies. Finding a place of contentment is challenging at times. We celebrate individuality, yet also want to look like the stereotypical, societal version of "good-looking."

As Glennon Doyle alludes to in the quote above, we are all in cages of some kind. It must be part of the human experience. The hope is that we do not have to live in the cages. If we look closely, the door to the cage isn't locked. We can simply walk out if we want to. Freedom is possible. Hopefully, this book will help you step out of the cages in which you feel imprisoned.

If you are supporting someone, it is important to remember all the facets of a person. We are not simple creatures. Some cultures believe that we are not just this person living on this planet, but we come with the history of our ancestors, with the karma of past lives. We are complicated in the most wonderful way. You will never experience something so wild as being in a human body walking through a lifetime. It is the only ride that leads you to beauty, both bitter and sweet.

Your parts are complicated. It is hard to reconcile all of it. Most of the time, we may even love ourselves, hate ourselves, think we are ugly and beautiful, good and bad, helpful and helpless, happy and sad, all in one day. Change is constant. It is okay to move through these things as they come and experience them, be curious, and let them pass like a cloud in a summer sky. If you deny yourself the ability to move through all that life presents, you will become stuck. Some will say you have not processed your experience and are not allowing yourself to get beyond it. If you stuff it down, it will bubble up. The only way to let it go is to work through it. The poet Rumi refers to our inner self as a guesthouse for all the emotions that come to our door, and says we should welcome them all to our table. Allow them to do what they will do, and then bid them goodbye. Welcome what comes, even if they are guests you don't want. There is no other way to be your true self than to address all the parts of you with love and kindness toward yourself.

5.

SOME THOUGHTS ON WELLNESS FROM DIFFERENT MODELS

*"There are many ways to look at an apple.
Some see a delicious dessert, while others see a thing
they traded away in the grade school lunch room."*

—Juliana Jay

While there are many modalities, therapies, rituals, and concepts around wellness, we cannot discuss them all. For our purposes, we will discuss two major therapeutic concepts and a few others from the more alternative approach. Again, there are many forms.

Somatic Practices

There are many different types of somatic work. Some will classify yoga as somatic work; some may even include running or working out. Other types might be more intentional. Somatic work is a balance of body and mind. These modalities are helpful because the body holds trauma as well as the mind. These practices utilize movement, touch, and articulation in conjunction with emotional work. Releasing the emotions and trauma held in your body will help you to let go of the narratives those events have anchored in your mind. In doing so, this action will allow you to create new narratives that are healing.

Some examples of somatic work are exercise, yoga, breathwork, voice work, dance, movement, massage, sensation awareness, grounding exercises, and somatic experiencing therapy, to name a few.

Practitioners work from the idea that trauma is not inherent in the event that caused the trauma, but rather, it is held in the mind and body. Trauma is held in your body and interpreted in your mind. Our relationship to the event causes the trauma.

This type of work can be very powerful. To get the results you do want, you do not have to work directly with your trauma; instead you work with the residue the event left on your body. If talking about past events is simply too painful for you at this point, you might consider somatic practices as a place to work with your trauma without having to talk about it directly.

Breathwork

Breathwork is simply using the breath to settle, regroup, ground, and recalibrate. Simple breathwork involves slowing down your breath and breathing deeply. One simple example is taking a deep breath in for the count of four, then holding it for four, before letting it out again for the count of four. Breathwork is often used in other modalities to help you to ground and feel centered—to create calming feelings or to center before or after you begin a practice or therapeutic work. It can be applied to your life in many ways. It can also be a stand-alone practice.

We all benefit from breathwork. Breath is the bridge between your body, mind, and soul. Using a few simple techniques when a situation presents itself can make a huge difference! Many people use breathwork before they present at meetings, or before they ask a question, or have a conversation, or drive to work, or get out of the car after work, or when the kids are out of control. Have you ever taken a deep breath before doing something a little scary? Like in the movies, when someone asks another to marry them, they often take a deep breath and then begin. That is a simple form of breathwork. Applying it on a bigger scale is incredibly beneficial.

One caution on breathwork. Sometimes, concentrating on your breath is not helpful. This can be true if you are suffering a loss of a loved one. I noticed this when I was grieving the death of a family member. Concentrating on my breath just reminded me of the body after death, not breathing. It was almost a trigger to a flood of grief followed by guilt—guilt that I was able to breathe, but my loved one could not. Even though I understand the spiritual aspects of leaving a body in death, the physical reminder was a challenge. As with all the modalities discussed in this book, move on to something else if it doesn't work for you right now. Come back to it when and if it seems valuable at the moment. What you feel today changes. What worked yesterday may lose its potency, and you must search for something else. It's part of the process.

Meditation and Mindfulness

Meditation and mindfulness are also extremely helpful modalities. These things have allowed me to heal in profound ways and continue to get me through rough situations. During the writing of this book, my beloved dog of fifteen-plus years, Pip, died. I am still stumbling through days with bouts of crying, laughing, breathing, crying again. I am struggling with the things that always accompany grief: blame, guilt, and twinges of all the times I wasn't there for her. The problem with grief is that hindsight will introduce grief to guilt. All the things I should have done, could have done, and wanted to do. Meditation and mindfulness have been a place for me to rest from feelings. It is a place to process things in a way that works for me. In the space of meditation and mindfulness, I understand that my feelings are part of being human. They are a choice on some level. I have the power to interpret feelings in more than one way. I also know that they pass. They may resurface now and again, but they pass. Meditation and mindfulness got me through the most challenging times of my life and have helped me work with everything life brings. Again, this work is something you can use throughout life when you need a friend to help you get through something or center you before you walk on.

Protective Intentions

The original idea for the concept of protective intentions is based on Protection Motivation Theory (PMT). It works with the idea that a person defines a threat by two factors: the appraisal of the threat itself and the coping appraisal. It is a theory of the mechanism by which a body perceives a threat and how it will protect itself. The intention of the theory is to predict what motivates people to change behaviors.

Often, this theory is applied to health-related situations—for example, the threat of a serious disease and how the patient will perceive the threat. This perception on the part of the patient affects their choices. People weigh their perceptions of their vulnerability and of the severity of the possible outcomes. Basically, we are talking about how likely a person feels that they may be affected by a disease, or habits that affect health, against the plausibility of death, pain, or other health-related concerns. Coping appraisals are your feelings on how you will engage in preventative measures. Response efficacy is at play here, meaning how sure are you that engaging in a particular behavior will have a positive effect. The person must also feel that they can engage in behavior that will help them. There is also a perceived response to healthy behavior. For example, a person may know that overindulging in certain types of drugs is a major health concern and may cause death, yet the payoff of escaping life for a bit is more powerful. The same is true for all of us who put off doctor and dentist appointments because we fear outcomes or that it will be embarrassing.

This theory works on our various fears about our health and how we respond to those fears and concerns. Using this theory, it is easy to see how people can be less incentivized to work on healthy habits because of the way they perceive health concerns and what they decide they should do.

If someone is very disenfranchised, they may ask, "What is the use?" This is a hard mindset to shift. This theory suggests that the patient must think there is a very real and dire threat, and that changing their behavior to a healthier one will diminish the threat significantly.

Internal Family Systems

Internal Family Systems (IFS), developed by psychologist Richard Schwartz, is a type of therapy that offers a model of three categories: exiles, managers, and firefighters. In this system, exiles are the part of our psyche that holds painful emotions, trauma, hurt, and shame from early experiences in life. They hold the difficult emotions and memories of those events. Managers try to keep control over feelings of vulnerability, which often results in harsh inner self-criticism. Firefighters try to stifle the exiles with external stimuli such as self-harm, addictions, and other behaviors that are damaging. IFS theory aims to use these models to learn more about the self and to better regulate our responses to painful memories and feelings.

In a sense, this modality works with seeing yourself (and people in general) as made up of different parts. This therapy is not for everyone, especially people who have a severe mental illness.

By accessing our exiles through a greater understanding of our emotions and physical responses, IFS therapeutic models work to help us understand and unburden ourselves from these exiles that are keeping us from the lives we want to have. A therapist will work with you, using talk therapy, to uncover your feelings around suppressed emotions and on how to then release them so that you can address the root problem about which the emotions were generated. Over time, this will help us to approach new situations in a healthier way. Much of this type of work involves techniques that are very common in other modalities, such as visualization, journaling, relaxation exercises, and even vision boarding.

I bring this to your attention to let you know that we all have exiles. You are not alone. This approach to understanding yourself through self-exploration and discovery can help you unburden yourself from the emotions that may be keeping you in the darkness. Perhaps they are not yet even known to you because they live in the suppressed spaces of your mind.

One Word of Caution about the Use of Healing Modalities

Healing modalities, therapies, and techniques are not to be used as a means to distance from people—to keep from getting into a deep relationship with someone, for example. I have seen many people, including myself, use things learned in therapy as tools to keep others at arm's length, as excuses not to engage in activities, and/or as excuses not to be there for someone or to witness hard things. These modalities are here to help you engage in an adventure to the self, to self-understanding, forgiveness, worth, love, growth, and any goal you have for yourself around healing. Most recently, I encountered a young woman who had suffered the loss of her sister. I observed that she tended to use phrases and concepts she had learned in therapy to stay distant from loyal friends she had had for years. She was eroding away the friendship instead of creating meaningful connections or working on parts of the relationship that might need attention. Although her loss was almost a decade earlier, and she had gone to therapy, she often left a therapist when they touched a nerve, said something that might have pushed her toward healing, or brought up a painful topic. She would apply the concepts she had learned to distance herself from others and to avoid hard feelings. Healing will present things you don't like. Some examples of this might be a view of your outward persona that you don't want to acknowledge, a change you must make to move forward, or an unfortunate incident that has become part of your self-definition in an unhealthy way. It could bring up regrets you have that have shaped negative self-talk. It might expose events you don't want to revisit. These things can be part of a healing process. Finding the courage to look at all of it is hard, but often needed. It isn't a place you go to where you get sympathy and admiration. Although that does happen in therapy, it isn't there just to please you and to give you tools to further degrade the beauty that you have in life. Many people spend years in therapy and just memorize what they hear, including certain things they can use to perpetuate the safety bubble they have erected to protect their inner child. The bubble may not actually be a protection at all. If you use a past event—however tragic and horrifying—to make people walk on eggshells around you, and you do so in the name of protecting your mental health, you aren't healing. You are masking. Healing is not about what is going on with others; it is about what is going on in your inner landscape and what is needed so that you can thrive in life. It is good to know when to retreat in order to rejuvenate. Using retreating as a mechanism for pushing folks away isn't rejuvenating. It can often be fear-based.

"What if I get in too close and that person leaves me?" "What if I tell them something deeply personal and they reject it or me?" It is fear that keeps you from healing. Fear that whatever happened may happen again. Fear that you will be judged. Fear that you will be "found out." There is so much fear for so many things. To heal, we need to become brave enough to face the fears, to be fearless when we turn inward, and to know that this fear isn't real; it is the body trying to keep us safe. The problem is that the body only responds in a black-and-white way. You are either in trouble or not, safe or not. It only sees internal pain as something to be feared, not to be healed.

Wellness Is Not a Destination

The path to wellness is not linear. You will encounter bumps in the road, turns, twists, crossroads, and wrong turns. Sometimes, you need to step off the path and rest. When you decide to seek wellness, or are supporting someone through their wellness journey, it is important to remember that this is a journey. It is not a straight upward trajectory from Point A to Point B. It will be more like a labyrinth or tangle at times. This is a process that involves addressing strong emotions, hard memories, and unhealthy patterns. It will include things like self-love, self-acceptance, empathy, compassion, self-regulation, and mindfulness. It involves hard work that is sometimes difficult to face. When working with your emotions, it is hard to tell if you have overcome something in the moment or if the work is long-lasting. It takes dedication to the work. It takes motivation and understanding. It takes being able to give yourself grace and time. It takes honesty and commitment. It is hard to rewire your brain if you don't fully engage in doing so. It will take getting out of your comfort zone. It will take being real with yourself and others. Supporting someone through this process takes compassion, empathy, understanding, patience, willingness to change, willingness to hear, deep, deep listening, and not offering advice unless it is asked for.

This journey will show you incredible vistas and beautiful sunrises, but it will also show you dark forests and vast deserts. So pack wisely, and when in doubt, remember that you packed loving awareness. Know that anyone can find themselves on this journey; we all use emotions to identify things in life. We all suffer.

Remember, people are not broken, though it can absolutely feel this way at times. A scientist friend of mine recently reminded me that context can define someone as having cognitive deviation. If the group thinks within the same process but an outlier thinks in different ways, they are labeled "different" or even "ill," yet if the same person were in a group of like-minded thinkers, they would be considered "normal."

Feeling broken is relatable. Sometimes you even feel physically broken as well as mentally struggling. This is normal. Your body responds to your mind, and your mind responds to your thoughts and emotions.

When you experience emotionally overwhelming feelings, your body releases cortisol, a chemical that causes more stress and anxiety. This can cause a depletion of serotonin, the chemical that helps us feel more grounded and calm and combats anxiety and sadness. As a result, we can be overcome with despair and feel a sense of hopelessness.

This results in feeling consumed by our emotional state. When you feel overwhelmed, it is hard to act and think rationally. We may feel like we have no control over our emotions, thoughts, and body. People with trauma may feel overwhelmed more often, and even at unpredictable times. This can be very painful and taxing, leaving us drained and unsure. Overwhelm can impact our lives, relationships, success, and ability to complete even daily tasks.

Folks who have experienced trauma often have a hard time regulating stress and factors that aid with or result in emotional overwhelm, because the ability to manage stress is compromised due to the trauma we experienced.

Overwhelm can feel like your body is letting you down. Even seeking help can be challenging, because our minds are so overwhelmed that we struggle to articulate our feelings and needs. Emotional overwhelm can trigger anger, fear, and anxiety, which in turn causes communication breakdown when you are trying to get help. It can manifest in health concerns, moments of panic, physical outbursts, tantrums, excessive crying, shortness of breath, chest pain, or rapid heartbeat and can even manifest as illness and unhealthy habits.

Depression and rage can be effects of unexpressed grief associated with loss (a death, a breakup, being let go from a job, and leaving school are common losses). Along with depression and rage, we may become hypervigilant and feel either detached or needy. When considering the five stages of grief, it is important to note that, while a fair amount of us go through the stages, some of us don't, or we skip over a stage. For example, if you experienced the death of a partner and had to just push forward because you had to support children or work more to make ends meet, you never took the time to truly grieve because there was no time. Or you tried hard to hide your grief from the rest of the family, and in doing so, you never truly had the time to go through your process. This is often true when there is a breakup or a loss on some other level. People around you may think you are overreacting, or you may feel embarrassed, so you stuff it down and walk forward in a daze. Never letting yourself grieve can manifest as various forms of anger, manipulation, rage, and so on.

Finding ways to work through this grief is important. Supporting people going through grief is also important. Grief is one of those things the world does not prepare you for, and thus we often don't have the tools to work through it or the language to support others. We feel uncomfortable or embarrassed, so we don't support others as we should. We may be having a hard time with the emotions of grief simply because we grew up in a family or society that did not tolerate crying or displays of emotion. So, when we are faced with loss, we don't go through the emotional stages of grief because we feel it is unsafe to do so.

We go through life hashing up this old unresolved grief every time a new situation occurs. Old grief crops up when you don't get a promotion at work or you have a negative situation in a relationship. It will keep presenting itself until you find closure.

Writing Exercise on Working with Closure

Finding closure is important. Many people write letters to those who have passed or left or even a boss, or they have an imagined conversation with them, talking out loud as though the person is there with them but cannot speak or react. What would you write to the person if you knew there would be no adverse effects, if you imagine that you would hand the person the letter and then walk away and never see them again? What would you say?

Attachment to Suffering

The Buddha said that the road to enlightenment is through understanding suffering. All people suffer. The cause of suffering is desire. Suffering does have an end. The end of suffering is found on the path to enlightenment.

Desires cause suffering. Sometimes, we want something we don't have; sometimes, we desire a different outcome or a different life; and sometimes, we suffer because we desire to live longer, to have more money, to have more of something, or whatever. Suffering comes out of perceived lack. We decide we lack something; maybe we don't have enough love, support, or kindness. Whatever it is, it is because of lack; thus, we desire something else.

Suffering is a product of the mind. We can let go of suffering because suffering is a construct we created. We can also choose to find peace in what is. We can decide to be proactive in getting what we want. We can let go of what others think we should have. We can let go of trying to be what others want us to be. Whatever it is, there is a path out of suffering. It might not be easy, but it is possible.

Sometimes, we become attached to suffering. Suffering becomes our comfort zone. We stay with suffering because we have made it part of our identity. For example, when we identify as being a loner or someone without friends, it becomes painful to have friends because they are out of our comfort zone, yet we want a friend very badly. We are choosing suffering over change. The comfort zone can be a dangerous place. It doesn't allow you to grow and change as your life grows and develops.

As with all the theories presented here, it is important to remember that acceptance is a vital part of healing. It is needed by both the person who is experiencing the emotions, thoughts, and feelings and the people supporting the person. Acceptance comes with realizing that everyone experiences anxiety, stress, sadness, and worry.

Although we are aware of therapy as a way to address many of these conditions, many different modalities are not as well known. We will discuss some of these later in the book, but a few are gaining popularity due to worldwide recognition and endorsements by prominent people in the wellness community.

These techniques include grounding exercises, meditation, working with the mind-body connection, breathing practices, mantras, affirmations, chanting, aromatherapy, energy work, yoga, and so much more. Not everyone walks the same path to healing. Many people participate in multiple modalities on the journey to wellness. Some take paths less traveled. It is really about finding what works for you and brings you happiness and a sense of hope and wonder.

There are many parts of you. Like the Rumi quote about the guesthouse, finding acceptance of what comes is essential to healing. Invite it all, try to see the gifts, and then bid it goodbye. Have compassion for yourself as you invite the hard-to-care-for into your guesthouse. Rejoice when the good things come to visit.

6.

COMPASSION PRACTICES

*"Be kind, for everyone you meet is fighting a battle
you know nothing about."*

—Wendy Mass, *The Candymakers*

While we will discuss compassion practices as exercises later in this book, it is important to know that there are many compassion practice models, from therapeutic models to spiritual and alternative practices. The basic premise is the same: find compassion for yourself and others. Many of these practices involve loving-kindness, meditations, breathwork, and the model of suffering from the Buddha:

- Becoming aware of your suffering.
- Finding sympathy and compassion for the suffering.
- Fostering a desire to ease the suffering.
- Taking action to ease the suffering.

The basic premise is to cultivate compassion through a more compassionate outlook, feelings, and actions. Compassion-based practices use the parasympathetic nervous system (the opposite of the one responsible for fight-or-flight responses) to encourage feelings of safety. It works not only to foster self-compassion, but also to be more compassionate toward others and to use compassion as resilience when under pressure. Fredrickson, Cohn, Coffey, Pek, and Finkel (2008) studied the effects of compassion meditation practices in relationship to emotional wellness and determined that those who practiced compassion meditation developed a more positive outlook on life.

Compassion practices shift attention away from your own emotions and depressive thoughts to another focus that is nurturing and caring.

Cultivating compassion deepens your connection to others, the Earth, communities, and enjoyable actions. Shifting to a mindset of putting positive energy out there in the world can be very healing. Compassion practices help create connections and can be beneficial to those feeling isolated or unloved.

Mindfulness and compassion practices can have the same effects and can also help you with your inner dialogue. Through mindfulness, you can shift your internal dialogue to a more compassionate voice. You can learn to forgive yourself more easily. For me, the biggest takeaway was that it allows you to be at peace with being imperfect.

A simple meditation practice for compassion is to use this Metta verse in a ten-minute meditation. Find a quiet place to sit or lie down, and set a timer for ten minutes. Close your eyes, soften your gaze, and take a few deep breaths to ground yourself. Then repeat the following over and over until your timer goes off:

May I be loved
May I be safe
May I be happy
May I be healthy

May you be loved
May you be safe
May you be happy
May you be healthy

May we be loved
May we be safe
May we be happy
May we be healthy

May they be loved
May they be safe
May they be happy
May they be healthy
May all be loved

May all be safe
May all be happy
May all be healthy

When you are done, rest for a moment in the words. Be thankful for having this time to practice, and when you are ready, go on with your day.

Reasons for Suicidal Ideation

According to the Mayo Clinic, suicidal thoughts are caused by many different things. But often, it is the inability to cope with an overwhelming situation. Your outlook on life becomes narrowed, and you can't see a way out of your suffering. You are feeling severe traumatic stress, and it can render you blind to all other things.

Certain drugs, such as antidepressants, may increase the odds of having suicidal thoughts. Substance abuse can also aggravate suicidal thoughts.

Again, it is important to take into account the factors we discussed previously. What may be a minor blip in life to you might be a traumatic experience to someone else. For example, children considering suicide can often be triggered by the loss of a friend or a bad grade, but an adult may not take these situations as dire.

Many different circumstances might lead to feelings of hopelessness. If you are caring for someone, it is important to realize that whatever the reason, it is heavy for the person suffering.

As I have already said (but it is worth repeating), only you can truly know the pain you feel. Only you can know the emotions, the memories, the context, the feelings, the headache, the fear, the anger, the grip of it. Only you. Even those of us who have been there don't fully know; we only know how we have felt.

Sometimes, we feel a deep sense of being misunderstood. Our society has not developed the tools to deal with anyone who is presenting outside of some narrow factors that make up "acceptable human behavior" for any given situation. If we are experiencing something that is uncomfortable for others, we often feel isolated and severely alone. We feel that no one understands us. That we must be the only people with these feelings. We emotionally kick ourselves for being unable to "snap out of it," whatever "it" is.

We are a species that requires community. We are hardwired to seek connection, and feeling as though we have no connections is isolating. I can't even find the words to express to you just how alone someone feels when they are not tolerated or understood. When, because of gender, lifestyle, culture, race, economic status, appearance, or family beliefs, you fall outside the boundaries of acceptable, you become isolated. Feelings associated with being unaccepted don't leave; they just stay there inside you, quietly asking if they can come out. Sometimes they come out when it isn't appropriate, and then you may feel the sting of shunning by a community you are trying to be a part of.

Due to this, we struggle with identity when trying to fit in. Who are we? Why are we here? Who do we belong to? Are we even worthy of the space we are taking up by being here? If we can't express these questions, we can find ourselves feeling as though our life has no meaning or value.

Sometimes, our life circumstances become intolerable. Fighting a disease or long-term illness, insecurity around food or housing or basic needs, losing everything, being stuck and unable to move, cognitive divergence, emotional divergence, loneliness, shame, guilt, self-hatred, feeling that world issues are too grave, fearing for your life and wanting to end it before violence happens, are just a few of the reasons we can decide that living has become too much. People outside of our skin may say, "Don't worry, it will pass," but we ourselves can't imagine it passing. How will it pass? We are often not offered a path to this "passing" business; we are just told to get over it, it will pass, another door will open... Okay, so I totally believe in the other door theory. It has happened numerous times to me, but when you are in the thick of it, that door is not visible. The door becomes visible when the better thing presents itself. It isn't there otherwise. Expecting someone to see that during a personal crisis is simply asking too much. It is jumping ahead of the issue, skipping over the current state of being. Often, this state of crisis has become part of our identity. Just asking us to give up that part of ourselves without any tools as to how and what to replace it with, and how to shift and be accepted, is asking too much.

It reminds me of when I had finally broken free of an abusive relationship—one I spent a decade in. One that shaped who I was simply because I thought that leaving was not acceptable. I complied because that is what I thought women were supposed to do. I also felt a great deal of shame, which was overwhelming. How I got out is another story, but I will tell you, it wasn't because I decided to leave. It was to save someone else. I didn't value my life enough to leave for me alone.

But once I left, I realized I had no fucking idea who I was. Believe me, an identity crisis doesn't just pass one day; you find a path out of it. You do the work to shift it. I didn't even know what foods I liked because I had been so controlled. I distinctly remember thinking to myself, "Do I like croissants? If I eat it, I will have to run four miles to burn it off because I am too big." Let me tell you right now, I fucking love croissants! But I was so programmed to associate anything I liked with being ugly and undesirable that I stopped enjoying the things that brought me happiness.

I did this not because I wanted to, but because I was manipulated into thinking it. I remember buying a cup of coffee and thinking it was the jackpot because I had never been able to buy coffee without permission. I was an ugly person, couldn't eat pastries because I was fat, couldn't spend money on anything unless given permission, couldn't be friends with anyone, and was a complete letdown to everyone around me. Even though these definitions of self were unfavorable, they were my definition of self, my comfort zone, and my security. It was hard to redefine myself, and I still carry many negative self-definitions around with me; they crop up now and again, depending on the situation. I had to work at this, though. I didn't just stop being these things without a process. I didn't see the door before it happened. I only knew that to survive, I had to shift.

Reasons for Completing Suicide

Reasons for completing include all of the above, and every other reason anyone on the planet can think of, but realize this: at the moment, you think it is the only alternative. Someone who has decided to complete suicide has already weighed out the alternatives and has decided this is all there is. Let that sink in. This is the only choice they have for you, for them, for the situation, for others. This is the only option. This is something they have been thinking about for a while. They may be so overwhelmed or suffering from other issues. They may feel that their problems are too big to fix. They may feel that this moment is all there is. They may feel that they will always be in pain and things will never change. They feel so alone and that no one really cares if they are here, alive. They may be crying out for help, but their cries go unheard. They feel intense emotions that cloud all other avenues for escape. They may even be experiencing unresolved trauma. Remember, trauma is specific to each individual; it cannot be judged by another. One thing that causes you great pain may only be an afterthought to me and vice versa. Leave the judgment at the door when you enter the space of support. It won't be needed there, and it will only hold you back. Here is a hard truth: if someone you love feels like their life doesn't matter, you are playing a role in crafting that belief. If you want people to feel valued, value them. Valuing folks is an act of support, understanding, and loving awareness. Judgment is an act of devaluing.

I find it upsetting when people call suicide a "selfish" act. It isn't at all. Often, it is justified in the mind of the person who is planning suicide as a way to alleviate the suffering they are causing others. They genuinely feel they are a burden, a barrier, a roadblock, a disappointment, a failure, someone no one wants around. They have decided that this action is a way to love. I know this is a tough one, but people frequently think leaving will make everyone else's life better. You have to understand that this is not a decision people come to lightly or on a whim. It may seem like it is because, as I have already said, when people reach out for help, they are often rebuffed or ignored. They hear things like, "Get over it," "You are making this worse than it is," or other such types of toxic positivity.

Part II

FOR THE PERSON CONTEMPLATING SUICIDE

*"As surely as there is a voyage away,
there is a journey home."*

—Jack Kornfield

We all journey away from ourselves at one time or another. We please others at the expense of ourselves; we try to fit in and pretend we are something we don't want to be. We fall prey to societal beliefs that we don't even agree with. We compete with folks who aren't even playing the same game as we are. We convince ourselves that we want things just because someone else has them. We feel alone, unloved, isolated, and rejected. We think we must be crazy because we don't think the way others do, or react the same way, or want the same things.

We lose ourselves in the making of our lives. It is often so gradual that we hardly realize it until we do. We become embarrassed or ashamed of what we have done or are doing. When things go wrong, we overthink everything and make our mistakes bigger than they are. Consequently, among other things, we feel unlovable and unworthy.

I get that; I've been there. I am still there some days, but now I am working on it. I believe this to be a lifelong practice, recognizing when you are not authentic to yourself and rerouting. It is also a lifelong practice to recognize negative self-talk and shift it.

It is possible to journey back to your true self—the self that you want to be, the self that you unapologetically are. Liking who you are is a pivotal component of this journey. You will need to travel to your own worth. You will need to realize that you are valid and worthy of love, dreams, joy, and so much more, my friend.

1.

YOU ARE LOVED— IT IS AS SIMPLE AS THAT

"Turning toward what you deeply love saves you."

—Rumi

Before I launch into all the science and theory of love, I want you to know that you are loved. People you don't even know love you. Folks are sending you love during their daily meditation practices, or prayers, or affirmations, or daily thoughts, or whatever they are doing. You are receiving love through the energy of others. You are also loved by people you do not yet know. Folks from whom you have never heard the words "I love you," but their actions speak their love daily. You are also loved by people who tell you they love you and by people you know well.

Beyond it all, know this: You are loved.

It is perfectly acceptable to desire love. All human beings seek love. We need not only to receive love, but to give it as well. Love is at the core of human experience. According to *New York Times* bestselling author and strategist Tony Robbins, love is a primal need. This means that without love, we cannot create community and connection with others. Without love, human development is hindered. Love is essential for the survival of human offspring. Love is critical for humans to thrive. Love can also be a physiological motivator, as outlined in a study by Enrique Burunat. According to Raj Raghunathan, PhD, in an article titled, "The Need to Love" in *Psychology Today*, love is directly related to our happiness. This is why love is so powerful. Love is one of the ways we define who and what we are. It is a benchmark we use to determine our worthiness. We ask ourselves such questions as, are we loveable? Are we worthy of love? Do we have love? Can we give love? Do we even know what love is?

These are all questions we ask ourselves when we feel lacking. Why do we feel lacking in love? It can be because we are not loved in the ways we would like to be loved. According to Dr. Gary Chapman's book *The 5 Love Languages: The Secret to Love that Lasts*, we all have different ideas of what it means to be loved.

That is to say that we all have different ways in which we like to receive love. Different gestures tell us that we are loved. For example, some people might feel that if someone helps them, they are loved, while another person may value receiving gifts more than help. Of course, it isn't this simple; many cues tell us we are loved, but sometimes, we may not get the affirmations as much as we would like, and we begin to feel less loved than we actually are. It might be that we have decided we are not loved because we feel shame, or worthlessness, or other feelings that hinder our ability to see both the love we have for others and the love we have for ourselves more clearly.

Try to remember this when you are looking through a jungle that you have constructed out of your own failings, mistakes, self-judgments, shame, and embarrassment. It is hard to see the love you have when your own negative self-talk obstructs the view.

Even if all you can see through the jungle of your own thoughts is a life you messed up royally, you are still loved. I promise you this.

I can also say that there is love waiting for you beyond this moment in time, this fleeting blink of an eye. I know there is love waiting for you. Do you know why? Because everyone on this planet wants to give and receive love. Look at all the dating sites out there. Everyone has a hunger for love. Giving love to others is one of life's greatest joys. This was illustrated by Harvard Business School professor Michael Norton and colleagues' research, where people were given an amount of money and asked to spend it on either someone else or themselves. The people who spent it on others derived more happiness than those who bought things for themselves. Loving kindness is a human need, both in giving and receiving.

Often, the most challenging love to accept is self-love. Loving yourself is critical. I am not talking about being self-centered or self-important. That isn't self-love. I am talking about acceptance, quiet and deep acceptance that you are worthy of your own love. This was a tricky thing for me to wrap my head around, and I still have issues some days.

We get used to our patterns and thoughts. They dig grooves in our brains like well-worn trails, like the grooves left by years and years of flowing water. When it rains, the water finds the groove and flows. This is how our thoughts work. We develop a pattern, a way of thinking, and those thought patterns pop up when an incident occurs. Like trying to make the water flow over the smooth ground, it will always seek the well-worn groove. It is the easiest path.

Self-hatred, unworthiness, and shame all wear a groove into your brain, and when a situation presents itself, you go to the emotion or self-dialogue that has the deepest grooves. Perhaps you often find yourself saying, "I am so stupid," or "I am not good enough." Consider the grooves that you are wearing with your internal dialogue.

We will work on shifting these grooves throughout this book. But for now, knowing what you are working with is enough.

Loving Practice:

- There is a saying that what goes around comes around. Try it for yourself and see how it works.

- Every day for the next month, give something to someone.

- It can be something as simple as a smile.

- It can be saying hello to a stranger on the street or holding the door open for someone in need. Whatever the gift of the moment is, simply give it.

Some people practice secret gift-giving; my mom did this on occasion. She would leave little gifts on someone's doorstep, in a suitcase, or on a windshield and not identify herself as the giver. She just gave random gifts without any expectation of thanks. She would randomly take you out for a special lunch for no reason whatsoever.

Whatever works for you, maybe you can combine the two practices, but give someone something at least once daily. I suggest you start small and work up to more. Perhaps you smile at one random person who walks past you. Once you get comfortable with that, do it more often. Maybe you work up to saying hello or giving a perfect stranger a genuine compliment.

2.

YOU ARE NOT ALONE

"If I'm such a legend, why am I so lonely?"

—Judy Garland

One thing that helped me when I was in a dark place was realizing that I was not alone. It was the loneliness that made me feel that being here wasn't so important to anyone else. Listen to me here: if you get one thing out of this book, know you are not alone. Whatever you think you did or whatever got you here, you aren't alone. Someone else has done that or been there, and thousands of folks are standing by your side right now. You aren't the only one who is here, in this place, and you won't be the last person to feel this way. It is okay.

You still aren't alone, even if you feel like everyone has forsaken you.

Judy Garland had mobs wanting to know her, be her, have coffee with her, and admire her, yet one of her lasting quotes involves her feelings of loneliness. Even Judy fucking Garland is standing beside you. You aren't alone.

You aren't alone in anything you have ever done.

You aren't alone on this planet.

You aren't alone in this town.

And you aren't the only one thinking what you are thinking.

You are part of humanity, and with that, you are part of 300 million years of modern human habitation on this planet. Currently, there are over eight billion other people on the planet.

Even so, we all feel loneliness at one time or another.

Some of us struggle with these feelings more than others. Some of us seek help from professionals or other health and wellness modalities, and sometimes the feeling passes. Sometimes, we feel profoundly alone; other times, it is just a feeling in the back of our mind.

These feelings of loneliness could be caused by a lack of deep connections with others. Even if we have lots of friends, we can still feel alone.

Sure, we like our friends and family and enjoy hanging out, but sometimes, we crave more profound and fulfilling relationships. In other words, we can have a lot of fun relationships but feel that no one really knows who we are. Sometimes, we feel we are actively hiding our true nature. We often hide who we really are because we feel others won't accept these parts of us. In doing so, we create separation from other people, which can lead to feelings of loneliness.

Similarly, perhaps we need help with being appreciated, noticed, or valued, or we feel that our knowledge or input needs to be valued. We may not be hiding who we are, but when we express our true nature or ideas, they are not received well or to the depth we hope for. This can lead to feeling devalued; simply feeling devalued can make you feel profoundly alone. Again, it is part of feeling that we are not understood and that the genuine parts of who we are aren't valued or cared about.

What brings on these feelings, and how can we think more deeply about shifting our mindset to one of belonging?

Okay, I want to come to you with the truth. I often feel profoundly alone, even within the confines of my own family home. Sometimes, I feel uncared for, unappreciated, devalued, and frankly, an annoyance. I keep thinking people will be kinder or more caring. But that is not necessarily the case. Currently, I am

writing this while I have COVID and am quarantined in a ten-by-
twelve-foot bedroom, where I have been for the last three days.
I am not going to lie. It has been hard. Especially because it is
winter break, and I have this whole week off from work, but I'm in
here sick. Tonight, I feel profoundly alone, even though people are
on the other side of my door. Then I think about everyone else out
there feeling alone, and I realize I am not. That keeps me here.

Feeling lonely can be a consequence of significant changes in
your life.

For example, you move to a new area or place and don't know
anyone, or you are starting something new, like college or
a new job.

Or maybe you are experiencing a breakup or a falling-out
with someone.

Your feelings of loneliness may result from living alone after
living with others for a long time or moving to a quiet town from
a bustling city. Even changing your commute can be a factor. Say
you used to commute on a crowded bus where you often saw the
same people, and you had casual relationships with some of your
fellow commuters, bus drivers, and even people on the street.
Now you drive yourself, and you don't see any of those people
anymore, and you miss them. Perhaps seeing the people on your
daily commute was somehow grounding, and now, even though
you are excited to drive to work, you are also missing them and
the feeling of routine.

Sometimes, even when you don't talk to someone, you can miss
their presence once they are not there. It is comforting to see
familiar faces, even if you wouldn't consider them "friends." For
example, when you went to school as a kid and saw the same

person at the front desk every day. It was expected, and it was somehow comforting. You didn't think of them as your friend, but you were happy they were there when you entered the office. You were glad to see a familiar face. They are there every day in quiet support of your daily routine.

Let's talk about things that can help you to feel less lonely.

These things can make you feel more connected to the world and the people you know, simply because they are comforting and supportive. They create value and meaning in your life, which, in turn, grounds you to have a greater connection with others and yourself.

Then there is the feeling that you have value. Often, older folks feel lonely because they feel others no longer value them. People don't care about their ideas or wisdom. They are treated as though they are outdated or "old school." Younger folks feel devalued because they lack experience or simply because they find themselves in more situations where authority figures dominate and hold power, like teachers and faculty in school systems or bosses at work. People with different lifestyles, cultures, ethnicities, social and socioeconomic statuses, or anything that makes them feel othered and different from the normative culture can sometimes struggle to feel valued.

Having close connections can make a difference. Having just one good friend who really knows you can make all the difference. However, sometimes, finding someone you can share a deep connection with is a challenge. It is hard to open yourself up to getting to know someone else. Often, we are so guarded that we do not let our relationships get deep. Sometimes, we are shocked when friends or lovers fade away after years of knowing each other. This can sometimes be an outcome when the relationship

becomes stagnant and a person is unwilling to deepen the bond
with the other person. There are many reasons not to deepen a
relationship with someone, but we also need to be open to putting
ourselves out there for that experience when it's possible and the
conditions are right.

Feeling comfortable with your surroundings, feeling safe and
cared for, and having your basic needs met are very important.
If you never know what is going to happen from one minute to
the next, then you are training yourself to be in a constant state
of fight or flight. In this state, it can be hard to deepen your
relationships, because you are always on alert, always waiting for
something terrible to happen. This will hinder your ability to get
close to people.

Feeling isolated and alone can be a problem. Even introverts need
human connection—some of us like to spend more time alone
than others. Being able to be with yourself and alone is vital to
your overall mental health, but you also need a balance. We are
animals that need social connection—balance your alone time
with spending time with others.

Sharing your interests with others is a good thing. Try working on
projects with people, volunteering to get involved, and joining a
meetup or group are ways to get out there after you have had the
alone time you need. Finding connections through commonalities
like causes, hobbies, interests, and likes can be an easy way to
connect with others without the pressure of making a one-on-one
connection right away. Finding a group of people who share an
interest can also help with feelings of belonging. Helping others
is profoundly satisfying and helps with finding purpose and
meaning in life.

Having friends who have time for you helps you establish worth and meaning. Nothing makes you feel lonelier than having friends who will blow you off when something better comes along or are untruthful when they want to get out of hanging out with you. If you have friends like this, consider doing less with them and more with new friends or with others who treat you with compassion and kindness. Sometimes, it is hard to get away from the friends who are treating you as a backup plan, because that type of manipulation is powerful! When it happens, you notice if it is a one-time issue of overbooking or a pattern of behavior. If it is a pattern, talk to the friend about it. If it continues, consider spending your valuable time cultivating new friendships. It isn't always easy to shift in this way, but it can be very fulfilling.

Having a relationship with someone who shares your interests and can be there for deeper conversations as your friendship deepens is very satisfying. When you are in a relationship with an emotionally challenged person or someone who has a hard time with intimacy, it can be hard to progress the relationship forward. Identifying someone who just can't go deeper is essential. You can appreciate them for what they bring to your relationship, but you can learn not to expect more from them.

Find people who listen and hear profoundly and respond with care. When you hang out with multitaskers who are texting others and zoning out when you are with them, you can feel significantly devalued over time. The relationship can get flat and one-dimensional. Again, talking to those who aren't fully engaged is a good first step. Maybe they don't understand how their behavior translates, or perhaps they are going through things too. If the lack of engagement persists, then realize that what you see is what you get. Enjoy what they bring to your relationship, but know they can't go deeper, at least not right now.

You deepen relationships when you share interests on a deeper level, not just curiosity or because everyone is doing it. When you are learning with people and growing as a person with others, you often feel deeply connected. Even if the situation isn't the most significant thing that has ever happened, people can make very close connections with others through shared pain or trauma. Being able to learn and grow and support each other, whether it is through a challenging breakup or learning French, learning and growing together creates a close relationship with depth.

All these things help create deeper relationships and deep connections, which are necessary for positive mental health. When you feel lonely in a group, it is often because your connection is not that deep. You may have even been through things with the other person, but if they haven't provided a safe space for you to be yourself, you will always be worried about offending them in some way. If that is the case, you will never live deeply into the relationship because you fear "getting in trouble."

That brings me to the last thing that keeps you from loneliness: having a relationship built on trust. Where you trust each other to come through, you count on each other, and you can be honest with each other. And this is hard. It is hard to find. Finding someone who will let you be you, flaws and all, is hard. It is, and many of us feel lonely because we haven't found someone we can be honest with. Someone who doesn't think our ideas or beliefs are too different, and someone who is okay with the fact that we are flawed and human and mess up some of the time. We need to find folks who get that. Who isn't holding us to a place of perfection we can't maintain?

Here are five things we can do right now to feel less lonely and create a connection:

1. Do something with other people: take on a project at work; join a class or workshop on a topic of interest, a book club, or writing group; or volunteer for a beach cleanup or a shift at an information booth.

2. Sit quietly in your home and think of all the other people around you doing the same. If you live in an apartment building, close your eyes and imagine your neighbors silently reading a book on the couch, making a cup of tea, drawing, or working, or doing exactly what you are. Imagine all of you going about your daily business, but with a connection to each other. Other people are there, whether they are on the other side of a wall or twenty miles away. Other people are there, doing exactly what you are doing or other parts of daily life, and you are connected to them. Do this for five minutes; set a timer. After a week, set the timer to eight minutes and increase over time to ten minutes every time you feel lonely.

3. Go somewhere crowded. The movies, a popular eatery, a busy shopping street, and a popular walking path. People watch. If you see someone with a scarf you like, tell them so. If someone smiles at you, smile back. If someone says "Hi" to you, say it back. Practice acknowledging folks who come in and out of your consciousness. Practice being in community with others and feeling connected. Say to yourself, "I am connected to these people. We are connected."

4. Help others. Volunteer, or hold the door open for someone behind you. Practice small acts of kindness over and over all day. Every time you see something, react. Help others and feel good about it.

5. Practice being the friend, lover, beloved, sibling, parent, or
    child you want to have. Listen deeply to the other person
    and remember what they say. Be what you want to receive.
    Be the friend you wish to have, but also be patient with
    yourself. And rest when you need to. You don't have to
    overdo it. Find a balance. Maybe that means interacting less
    often but more deeply. Perhaps it is finding time for more
    one-on-one interactions vs group activities, or maybe it
    means visiting for shorter times but more often. You know
    what you need.

3.

YOUR PAIN IS VALID

*"Behind every beautiful thing,
there is some kind of pain."*

—Bob Dylan

Regardless of what anyone else may say, your pain is real. You have every right to feel whatever you feel. Don't stop talking about it; don't let others silence you, even if you tell it only to yourself and the wind. Do not let anyone tell you what you are feeling and then judge it as valid or not. If you feel it, it is valid—end of story.

Your pain does not mean you are worthless.

Your pain does not have to make sense.

Your pain should never be judged using the yardstick of extreme circumstances.

Comparing pain to other incidents worldwide, or that have happened to other people, is not a valid way to gauge pain. None of it is relevant to this pain you have. Your pain doesn't have to be rated on a scale to be worthy of attention from others. Care and compassion are not withheld from you if your pain isn't rated high enough on the tragedy scale. Your pain is not a burden to others. Your pain is inherent in the process of living. No one escapes it. We all experience pain.

The notion that if you feel pain, you are somehow acting like a baby is ridiculous! Facing pain is one of the bravest and strongest things a person can do. Why do you think so many people ignore it or stuff it down? Because facing your pain and reaching out for help takes guts, strength, and bravery.

People will not be crushed under your pain. We can handle it.

Make no mistake; sometimes, the pain will be close to unbearable. It will take you by the neck and strangle you. It will inflict physical pain on every space inside your body. Your skin will burn, your eyes will ache, your muscles will cry out, and even your bones will shudder under the weight of sorrow. It is hard. I know. If I could hug you right now, I would because, dear one, you are not alone in this pain. You are not weird, or incapable, or deranged, or psychotic. You are human. Humans hurt sometimes. No one escapes pain, no one. We all suffer in different ways, with different things, at different times.

People want to help you. They may not know how, but they want to help you. It is just that pain is taboo in a lot of families. When we fail to talk about pain, we never develop the skills to support people to move beyond pain. Often, the first response you get is anger, not because people are mad at you per se, but more because people are mad at themselves for not knowing what to do immediately. They deflect the anger onto you because that is what they have learned to do. They are angry for feeling uncomfortable with your pain, for not knowing the right thing to say or do. This is why it is a good idea to think about what you need, so that you can tell people how to help you.

Exercise on Exploring Pain

Label your pain. Example: I feel so alone that no one will miss me if I am not here.

How can people help you with this pain? Do you even know? Sometimes we don't. Sometimes, we don't know what we need from moment to moment. But we can identify things like someone to listen to me, someone to notice when I am sad, someone to check in on me, someone to help me get professional help, someone to drive me to the therapist. Give people clear ideas of how to help because sometimes, when they take it upon themselves to help you, they may do the wrong things.

4.

—

YOUR JOY IS VALID

"Life doesn't have to be perfect to be filled with joy."

—Anonymous

Joy, grief, sadness, and despair can coexist inside of you, along with everything else you experience. When I was in the depths of depression, I remember feeling guilty about any joy I experienced. I stuffed it down because I was honing sorrow and not cultivating joy. Over time, when joy cropped up, it was unexpected, and I had almost forgotten how to enjoy it. It felt like a luxury I wasn't allowed to have. It was almost like I was doing something wrong or naughty if I was joyous. I wasn't worthy of joy.

Joy was something I was waiting to feel when I came out of the dense fog of sadness that I had wrapped myself in. It felt like a reward I would get if I behaved and decided to be like everyone else. I will let you in on a secret here: everyone else is you. All the other people out there have emotions that are not acceptable in pleasant company. All the other people out there have things happen to them that bring up feelings of shame, loneliness, despair, regret, embarrassment, or whatever. Remember, you are not alone. This thought of being weird if you have feelings is a societal construct that we have all fallen into. Some sort of macho or "cowboy up" belief we subscribe to, even though it isn't serving any of us. It is not weak to have feelings. It is profoundly human and part of the human experience.

Your joy is not a prize you get if you are good at healing. Joy is yours, always. You own your joy. It can't be taken from you and parceled back out to you when you are "good" or "behaving well." Your joy is your fucking joy. You own it.

Joy is found in the moment of now. You can look back on moments that have now become fond memories and feel joyous, but feeling joy can only be experienced in the present moment. It isn't something you once had or may have again; it lives inside you at this moment.

- It is your right to feel joy and to feel sadness two seconds later.
- It is your right to be joyous when you feel good about yourself.
- It is your right to feel joy when you see a heartwarming commercial.
- It is your right to feel joy for others.
- It is your right to feel joy for yourself and all you have done, will do, and are doing.
- It is your right to feel joy whenever you damn want to!
- It is your right to feel joy and not feel bad about it.
- Your joy is valid. PERIOD.

Living with Your Joy Practice

Find a quiet, safe space to relax.

Get comfortable.

Close your eyes and take three long, deep breaths.

Now, imagine your joy as a beautiful mist or liquid. Maybe it is your favorite color. Imagine that this mist wraps around you and hugs you in a warm embrace. Imagine the mist accompanying you everywhere; it never leaves your side. When something happens that pleases you, the mist of joy erupts, cheers, and hugs you.

Imagine other people trying to take it, but when they do, the mist goes through their fingers right back to you. Your joy is loyal only to you. It always comes back to you; no one else can take it because it escapes every time.

Imagine each person you feel has tried to take your joy, imagine them trying to take it again, and imagine your joy flowing right through their fingers back to you.

Imagine your joy materializing. Imagine it waiting to validate you. Imagine it as a loyal friend and ally.

Imagine it always with you.
Imagine it loving you and being there for you.
Imagine the times your joy has been there for you.
Imagine future times when joy will be there.

Feel joy inside your body now, wrapping you in a warm blanket and laying its head on your shoulder. Feel this sensation until you are ready to open your eyes.

Do this whenever you feel disconnected from your joy.

5.

EVERYTHING IS TEMPORARY: A MEDITATION ON CHANGE

"Nothing is permanent except change."

—The Buddha

The only thing I know for sure is that there is only this moment right now. I can't say the next moment will be the same, but I know that it will change sooner or later.

Everything changes, like the seasons, the weather, childhood, and the taste of tea as it steeps. How you feel right now will also change. I know it seems wild, but it will.

Change will be good, and it will be bad, like a good haircut or a bad day at work. Everything is in a state of flux.

People often think certain things are fixed and permanent in life. These can include housing, relationships, jobs, friends, and economics, but the truth is that everything is impermanent and in flux. Even a mountain that has been here since the Ice Age has changed and continues to change with every passing season.

Expecting something to be permanent creates a lot of conflict and suffering when things change. Many of us find ourselves clinging to the idea of permanence because we find comfort there. It is less work if everything stays the same, but we don't think about how boring it will be if everything stays the same. Learning to flow through change helps alleviate suffering. Thinking about change as something exciting rather than challenging helps you to better navigate the unpleasant when it arrives.

When you open up to the notion that everything is constantly changing, you open a space for possibility. If you can wrap your mind around it, impermanence is infinite potential. You do not have to stay as you are today. You can be anything. This state is not permanent; it will pass, and something else will present itself.

People are conditioned to dislike change, but it can also be the best thing that ever happened to you. Even the best moments in life would not be as wonderful if they were stagnant and unchanging. We all need the ebb and flow to give us context. Without the good things in life, we would be unable to identify the not-so-good things. We need the concept of change to understand the world we live in.

I want you to know that change will come. Your perspective will change. You will have good days and bad days and "meh" days. Life will cycle through all the spaces there are.

Today, someone told me something hard to hear in a very uncompassionate and cutting way. It was hard to hear, and I felt attacked. To be honest, I have felt for a while now that I must walk on eggshells with this person, and it was hard to be direct with them. They will often come to me with direct and hurtful observations, and to be totally honest, I have grown scared of interacting with them. They also come from a place of being more right-minded than me, so interactions with them can either be enjoyable or cutting. Today, it was a cutting-to-the-core type of exchange. It was a compassionless interaction that left me a complete wreck. After crying in the fetal position (yep, for real) and texting a close friend, I was able to move on. My thoughts about this crisis included running away, hiding, moving away, being distant, and finding activities to keep away from them. So, I realize this is my go-to, escaping when things get tough, so I have been working on it and am trying to stay with things more. But in a brief moment of about two hours, some extreme change happened; I went from making spaghetti to crying in my bed with the covers over me to writing this passage. Maybe next week, I won't even be thinking about this anymore, but right now, I am raw with it all. Things change.

Sometimes, it is hard to get humans to change. Honestly, that is their work, and if they are not interested in change, then there is not much you can do except to change your perspective. You can only do what you can do; you can't be the change for others. You can, however, work on your expectations or your own behavior. You do have the power to change that. If you find yourself in a situation like this, change your thought patterns about it. I don't say this lightly, because it isn't easy, but it is possible.

Finding Peace with Impermanence Exercise

Make a list of three to five things that are causing you pain, leaving ample space between each item and the next.

Take item 1. Say it is "living in this house." Make an arrow —> and list an alternative, say, "moving out to an apartment on my own." Make another arrow —> coming out from the item, and list another alternative, such as " staying here but doing more things outside of the house" and another —> to "not relying on the people I live with for entertainment or companionship as much." Do this again and again until you have exhausted all ideas. Your alternatives should be fairly realistic.

Go to items 2, 3, 4, and 5 and do the same.

Notice that something you thought was so permanent actually has a lot of alternatives.

Are there any alternatives you can start right now? Are any of the other options something you can work into a future goal? For example, if I am "moving out," I could start saving money and researching possible places to move to so that I can move when I have enough money saved and the circumstances are good. Sometimes, just having a plan to move beyond the issue can be very comforting.

6.

——

MOVING FORWARD
IS NOT LINEAR

"Babe—healing isn't linear.
And look how far you've come."

—Laura Jane Williams, *Our Stop*

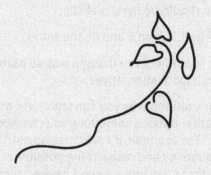

Martin Luther King Jr. referred to forward movement as encountering a mountain on your way to the glimmering city. Due to the rugged terrain, you must travel around the mountain, but in doing so, you lose sight of the city. It feels like you are going backward, but in actuality, you are getting closer.

Some days, you will still have moments. There will be mistakes, wrong turns, big snafus, and minor glitches. *C'est la vie!* That is life. It isn't perfect.

Life is made up of fleeting moments of perfection, and the rest is filled with other things. Perfection isn't necessary to have a joyous and rich life. In fact, you never need to be in a state of perfection to have a fantastic life. A state of perfection is a myth. I have found that perfection is a brief encounter. It is a moment when the sun hits just right for all of thirty seconds before it moves on. The skill is in registering the brief moments of perfection and soaking them in.

We will come across significant loss, trauma, and challenges over and over in life. Learning to be resilient is essential for this journey. Often, I have thought, "I'm cured!" only to be back in the depths of it as soon as I have a negative social experience. You may not ever completely move beyond what hurts. It will heal with time, but it may leave a nasty scar. Even with these scars, you can still have joy, happiness, love, and a fantastic life. In fact, the scar may lead you to the fulfillment you are searching for. I know that is hard to see right now. For now, just know it may be possible. Remember what I said about coming to this book with openness, and let this notion find a place in the edges of your mind. "This scar may lead me to the fulfillment I am searching for."

Living with your beautiful and mysterious scars with grace and joy may seem like an impossibility. There is an anger, a sorrow, a regret that clouds the view. Some of us have learned to see those scars not as regrets or ugliness but as life-changing and deeply human moments in life. Many of us with scars end up holding them in a sacred space. Not as martyrs, but as a looking glass that gave us new perspectives on life. Perspectives of which we were unaware. Unaware of it until the scar. I also know this to be true because I am living this example. I wouldn't be living if not for the tools we discuss within these pages. You may never be a fun-loving goof, but my guess is that isn't your goal anyway. On the other hand, maybe you will be. Only you know.

For me, most of the moments of perfection I have experienced have never even had to do with just me. Often, it is perfect lighting on the ocean in the early morning, a perfect moment at a concert, or seeing a whale while gazing out over the water. Once, a sea otter with her baby came right up to me while I was on my surfboard and hung out for a while. It was a moment of pure perfection. We don't live in a space of perfection; we simply get a glimpse of it occasionally. As I said above, when you glimpse it, take a moment to honor it, live deeply into it, notice it, and let it sink deeply into your heart.

In mindfulness, we are told to notice something beautiful in nature but not to name it. For example, if you see a beautiful flower, notice it deeply but do not say to yourself, "Wow, that flower is beautiful," because in doing so, you have taken your concentration off the flower and into your internal dialog. Instead, just notice it without defining it or judging it. Just notice. Try this mini-meditation when you feel that you need a pause. Even in a meeting room or classroom, you can find beauty. Take a few seconds to notice it, take a few deep breaths, and deeply notice, but don't define it. This exercise will take under a minute. Try it on for size.

Perfection isn't needed for forward movement. The only thing you need is the ability to keep going. The ability to get back up and dust off, and—okay, that is fucking hard to do, by the way. I am sure you know this. Getting back up is especially hard if you feel embarrassed, or ashamed, or stupid, or whatever. It is fine. We have all been there and will probably be there again. Just stand back up. If you need help, let this book be a hand that reaches out to you. If you need a minute, take one. Maybe you take all night if you need to. Then, stand up. I am not saying solve it all. I am saying that you possess the power of resilience. You know you possess it. Let it rule this moment. Just stand, and work on the rest later.

So, take a day to stay in bed and recover if that is what is needed. Be good to yourself; give yourself grace, space, and time. Cry, kick, and scream, and do it some more. Sing at the top of your lungs to your sad song playlist. Sob loud and ugly, and then laugh your ass off for no reason. Start planning your next move, smile at your idea, and start again. It's kind of the wash, rinse, repeat situation, except that sometimes the rinse cycle will vary depending on your turns and back steps. You may need to pre-rinse or use some stain remover, but everything comes out in the wash...eventually.

You are worthy of healing, love, and happiness. Don't forget that. If you need a reminder, write it on a Post-it and keep it handy so that you can look at it when you feel disillusioned. Sometimes, it is hard to accept our own love. Use a Post-it until it becomes real. Like the Velveteen Rabbit, sometimes all your fur must be loved off and you lose an eye, before you know you are real.

Two more myths worth mentioning:

- Straight lines are a myth (they do not exist in nature, so they say).
- "The right way is the only way" is a myth because there are an infinite number of ways.

Love Letter Exercise

Write yourself a love letter for when your future self feels stuck. Tell them how proud you are of them, how much you love them, and tell them how great they are doing. Encourage them to keep moving forward. Sign it with "I love you."

7.

—

EXPECTATIONS OF OTHERS

*"I hope you do not let anyone else's expectations
direct the course of your life."*

—Julianne Donaldson

While I adamantly agree with Julianne Donaldson here, I also know how hard it is to let go of trying to please people and living up to the expectations of both yourself and others. When I was fifteen years old, I got pregnant. I knew this would be a massive disappointment to my parents for so many reasons, and I was right. The dread of disappointing them was like a thick layer of gray mud that sucked me down deeper every time I took a step toward telling them. I can't fully explain the experience to you in a way that would do it justice. Suffice it to say that that was my first experience with contemplating ending my life.

The dread left me years later when I moved out of my parents' house, but the scar of letting them down seemed only to fester. I had not yet gathered the tools to work on the shame and unworthiness that I felt by letting them down. I lived with that pain for decades, until one day, the phrase "You are enough" seeped out from the confines of my mind and flowed into my body. Only when I understood that phrase with every cell in my body was I able to let go. How did I do this? It was a simple question from a friend; she asked me, "Juliana, you are enough just as you are right now; why do you think you have to do something more before you can be enough?" That was all it took: another human being honestly telling me that I am enough just as I am.

There is something about the difference between intellectually understanding the words and letting their power flow deep inside you. Letting the knowing present in each word wash away the feelings that define you as lesser than or not worthy. At that moment, as I contemplated the question, I began to cry. I was releasing all the years of holding onto the idea that if I could only be something more, then I would be enough.

All this is to say that the judgments of others are very powerful, especially if they are from people who are close to you or whom you love and/or admire. With that said, you do not have to let them shape your own views of yourself. You do not have to view their expectations as universal truths or standards that everyone else is following.

The other thing to remember is that everyone disappoints themselves or others sometimes, everyone makes mistakes occasionally, and everyone has a contrary viewpoint or a differing opinion to another. *Everyone.*

Life is not lived in perfection; perfection is a myth. It only exists in minute moments as a perfect moment in time. It is not a word to describe a human. Scratch the surface of any person out there, and you will uncover the beauty of imperfection. That is what makes us all unique and interesting. Our ability to be different, to suffer, and to move through our suffering may not make us perfect, but it makes us beautiful.

Exercise on Discovering Your Expectations and Beliefs

Make a list of your expectations for yourself. Now, do a deep dive. Are these your expectations or someone else's? How do these expectations match up with your values and beliefs? Are you in sync with your authenticity?

What would your expectations be if you simplified them down into a set of three expectations (one to three sentences each)?

8.

YOU ARE THE ONE YOU'VE BEEN WAITING FOR: PRACTICES FOR HOW TO BE THERE FOR YOURSELF

"If you have the ability to love, love yourself first."

—Charles Bukowski

In this section, we are going to talk about nurturing yourself and parenting your inner child if needed. It is about doing the things that you may feel you should have gotten as a child but maybe never did. Learning how to self-parent involves nurturing and caring for ourselves just as a small child would rely on a caretaker. Fostering a community of nurturing each other begins with nurturing ourselves. Learning to rely on yourself involves learning the techniques and skills needed for healthy caretaking.

Often, some of these nurturing practices are woven into what we call self-care. Self-care practices, such as deep conditioning your hair or applying a face mask, are part of taking care of your body, much as we do for children in the form of bathing them, washing their hair, or helping them brush their teeth. It has an element of compassion and care along with satisfying basic needs.

Part of being there for yourself is finding a place of safety. What does this mean? Well, many things, from your physical surroundings to how you interact with your inner self. Do you need to employ self-parenting models? Do you need to work through unresolved trauma? Do you need to distance yourself from toxic relationships or situations?

It is crucial to find a place where you feel safe. If you have a safe place at home or work, make it beautiful. Add some comforting things; maybe it is a soft blanket, reducing clutter, listening to music you enjoy, or just deep cleaning your space every once in a while. Surround yourself with books you like or sayings you find nurturing. Whatever it is, create a sanctuary where you can go to relax.

Reduce stressors in your life. If you are strongly affected by your news feed, consider having days when you do not look at it. News-free days can become your safe days. Let go of people in your life who are making you feel unsafe. You do not have to engage in relationships that are not healthy. You can determine that the relationship is positive overall, but some of the interactions feel unsafe. If so, what are those interactions? Is there a way to work on boundaries around those interactions that will help you? Or is there a way to work out this issue with the person? Develop a game plan for when the interaction becomes unsafe for you. Maybe it is a person at work who always unloads their negative viewpoints about life, or they always unload all of their problems, leaving you drained and overanalyzing your own life. If you can't stop them from doing that, consider how you can change your perspective on their rants. Can you shift your response to their anger as not something scary, but simply their reaction to themselves? It has nothing to do with you.

If it makes you feel better, I am constantly working on this. To me, anger is scary. If it catches me off guard, I find myself feeling as though I am in danger. My fight-or-flight response kicks in. Lately, I have been working on self-soothing by talking myself off the ledge—reminding myself that the anger is not about me, nor is it directed at me. I don't have to engage with the anger; I can walk away. I can tell this person that I am triggered by rage, but I want to help them and then ask them how I can help. I can decouple my past traumas associated with anger from this current experience by telling myself this is not happening in that timeframe; it is different. It is about reassuring myself, just as my mom would do if I were frightened at the playground. I would trust her to hug me tight and say everything was okay or to keep me safe if there were a real threat. It would be best if you found ways to do that for yourself, to soothe yourself when needed and keep yourself safe when needed. It is essential to realize when you are being triggered and surround yourself with safety, just as you would expect from a functional caregiver.

Understand what you need to feel safe. This will involve some self-parenting. What do you need to feel safe? Make a list, and then consider how you can provide that for yourself. Ask yourself, what does my inner child need? What didn't I receive as a child? Now, ask your adult self to give that to you. Ask your adult self to give your inner child the things that you didn't get as a child but needed to feel safe. For example, perhaps you needed acceptance when you were little, but you were not given it unless you acted as others wanted you to. Acceptance was conditional on things that weren't authentic to you. Now that you know, you can give that acceptance to yourself in the form of self-talk that reassures you that you are enough just as you are. You are accepted.

Finding self-worth and worth in others: sometimes, this concept is referred to as dignity. Dignity is inherent in all of us. It is intertwined with our deep need to be valued. We all have a need to be valued, heard, understood, and included. When we realize that others also feel the same, we can meet one another in the space of mutual understanding. Dignity is not so much about respect, although many of us associate dignity with respect. Rather, the two concepts intertwine. Dignity is something you are born with. It is a feeling of self-worth and self-value. It is also about seeing the worth and value of others. Respect is something usually offered by another person. You tend to rely on others to get respect. The truth is that respect starts with you. You do need to respect yourself. Respect your own boundaries and respect yourself enough to keep safe, cared for, and balanced.

Dignity is a helpful concept to apply in relationships. It is about realizing that you and the other person have a desire to be valued, seen, heard, understood, and included. This allows you to find compassion and empathy for each other. Dignity will enable you to say you're sorry in a meaningful way. If you understand the other's basic dignity, you realize that they are just trying to find worth.

When you hear someone say they are sorry, you realize that they are seeing your dignity and acknowledging your worth. Being able to be genuinely sorry and to express it to someone is powerful.

I was in a relationship with someone who had a tough time saying sorry, and when they did, it was in a sarcastic tone and/or always went like, "I am sorry, but you..." Over time, that inability to say sorry was a major factor in ending the relationship. I always felt so misunderstood and devalued. I realize now that it was because they never acknowledged my humanity in a way that made me feel seen. It sent a silent message to me that I was not valued. In hindsight, I often wonder if that inability to say sorry was a result of their failure to see their own dignity, as though their own lack of self-worth was reflected in how they treated others.

Do you desire to be heard, included, seen, acknowledged, and treated fairly and compassionately? This fact tells you that you have dignity. The trick is to realize it and live into your dignity by seeing it in others and yourself.

Perhaps you can start this practice by doing one thing every morning. When you wake up, look in the mirror, into your own eyes, and say to your reflection, *I am worthy. I am enough, and I claim my birthright of dignity.*

Belonging is part of that dignity concept we were just talking about. It is about feeling included and connected and feeling like others appreciate you. Belonging is so essential to our overall satisfaction and happiness. We are, by nature, a communal species. Without the community of our family or caregivers, we would not survive childhood. Belonging is part of our wiring. We are programmed to desire to belong because it keeps us safe and alive. So much of our self-worth and identity is tied up in our thoughts on our belonging. If we feel we don't belong, we may feel inadequate or unloved.

We may belong to a group that is much different from us, like a group of folks who don't think like us or act like us or believe in the same things we do, and yet we belong. We find a shared space to occupy.

Belonging gives us a sense of worth and legitimacy. Community and belonging are partly how we shape our identity. Belonging helps us feel like we have a purpose in the world. Belonging can significantly reduce stress because we know we have people we can go to for support. We feel that we will be understood. It helps us feel connected and less lonely. It helps ground us to the places and identities we hold. It gives us a place of safety. It lets us know that we are understood, valued, appreciated, and enjoyed and that we matter.

Many of us are part of communities because we were born into them, or our parents were part of them, or it had to do with school or work. We may be part of these groups, but do we feel like we belong? Feel connection? If we don't, why? If we do, what connects us? Belonging is not just about your communities; it is about feeling included, understood, supported, cared for, and loved. Belonging creates motivation, which is the key to happiness.

Who do you belong to? What groups and/or communities? Once you start thinking about it, you can see that you are part of many communities. Consider how you find belonging in those groups. For example, many people who are not out might identify with LGBTQIA+ groups/communities, but not be actively engaging with the groups. Possibly, there is fear around being found out or that their current groups will not accept them. Take a moment to think about how you engage with the groups you identify with. Why are you or aren't you engaging with these groups? How could you find belonging?

Practicing belonging by looking for ways you overlap with people, the commonalities you share, the connections. Start training yourself to see connections rather than factors that make you different from others. Work on seeing other people's points or understanding your differences. Again, remember the dignity factor. Listen to opposing views, and remember to come to the conversation in a space of mutual dignity and understanding. Leave judgment at home when you connect with others. Judgment is an isolation tool. It can make you feel superior for a moment or two, but the long-term effects will leave you feeling isolated and alone.

Work on using inclusive words and not concentrating on illustrating differences. Remember, there is no need to bring judgment to the mix. Find commonalities rather than differences. Be open to others' opinions and thoughts. Develop compassion and empathy for others. Become an ally rather than an opponent. Be forgiving, but don't be a doormat. Have good boundaries, but be open to the boundaries of others. Go out on a limb and try things you have been curious about. Maybe it is a meetup, or taking up group guitar lessons. Perhaps you join a rec league, a drumming circle, or a yoga class.

Belonging is about being inclusive, so practice acceptance and understanding. Be curious.

You already have your answers, and/or you know where to find them. This is about tapping into your inner wisdom. Your intuition. We have all experienced the wisdom of our inner knowing. Inner knowing is the vast field of exceptional knowledge that you possess. Just think about this for a second; look at the things you have learned since infancy. From day one, you have been learning, taking in stimuli, working it over in your mind, and learning how to apply it to daily living. Now, think about everything you have intentionally learned just because you were interested in something. It's incredible! All that knowledge and the ability to use it to extrapolate and theorize on unrelated events. It is like watching someone peel an orange and then instinctively knowing that other fruits may also have a peel. Or learning to walk and then knowing you can apply the same concept and run.

You have a wealth of knowledge and experience. Think of this wealth as a deep working of your inner knowing. Knowing resides in a deep, bottomless well of information and wonder. Your inner wisdom is endless and all-knowing, but it is also burdened—encumbered by societal expectations, emotions, and memories, all the time. Maybe someone told you that you were doing it wrong, you were stupid, or you got in trouble. These things shackle our inner knowing and prevent us from tapping into our best judgment. Often, people are so concerned with what others might think of them that they shut off their inner knowing altogether.

Often, your body will cue you. Have you ever broken into a sweat when you were about to do something you knew you shouldn't be doing? Or maybe it was a racing heart (not in a good way, but in a wrong way). Those body clues, combined with a general unpleasant feeling you can't put your finger on, is your inner wisdom talking. Have you ever felt a rush of adrenaline (in a good way) that plants a genuine smile on your face right before you are about to do something new and exciting? That is your inner voice saying, go for it! Now is your chance! There's more to your inner wisdom than using it as a guide. It is a place to rest. To recharge. It is your inner place of safety. Know that it is you seeing, acknowledging, and knowing that you are worthy and that you matter. Go there when you are looking for sanctuary. Realize you always carry it with you. You always have a sanctuary to rest in, no matter where you are.

Using and acknowledging your inner wisdom is a great way to work on developing trust in yourself and your choices. Working with your inner wisdom helps you strengthen the connection to yourself, your beliefs, your ideas, and your purpose. It helps you connect with your authenticity.

Working with your inner wisdom is easy. Just take a few moments to ground and connect with yourself every day. Listen for signs of your inner wisdom showing up within yourself, in your thoughts, and out there in the world. In the book *Signs: The Secret Language of the Universe*, Laura Lynn Jackson discusses all the ways the universe speaks to us, from songs, lyrics, and images to numbers, feelings, thoughts, and so on. Your wisdom is connected to the wisdom of the universe, and by simply paying attention to what speaks to you, you can tap into a deeper level of understanding that will vastly improve your feelings of security, trust, and self-reliance.

Inner wisdom can help you to receive the hard parts that come. Reframe these hard things in a way that makes them less scary and more acceptable. It becomes not, "Why does this always happen to me?" but rather a, "Well, here we go, how can I work through this?" attitude. It aids in your resilience. Resilience is a powerful tool that can redirect your life. Classic examples of resilience can be found in people who lost it all and built it back up. I am not suggesting this is easy, or that even building up what was there before is the best option, but resilience allows you to roll with things a little easier. It helps you to reframe negative outcomes not as defeats or crippling factors in life, but as tools and opportunities. Resilience allows you to look beyond the current situation and find new ways of doing things. It helps to foster feelings of worthiness and self-love. You foster self-soothing and self-reassurance. When needed, use the mantra, "It is going to be okay." It may sound simple, but it can be beneficial as you work with your resilience.

Practice on Fostering Self-Love and Inner Knowing

Sit quietly and close your eyes. Take a few deep, slow breaths. Settle into yourself. Imagine that you have roots, and those roots are burrowing deep into the ground; you can see the dirt moving as your roots go deep into the earth, grounding you and providing safety.

Once you feel safe, it may take a few minutes, but once you are safe and grounded, bring your breathing into your heart. Imagine breathing in and out through your heart. Imagine the love in your heart growing bigger and bigger until it becomes a golden bubble all around you. Feel the love for yourself in the bubble, warm like sunshine, safe, soft, kind, just right. Now say "I love you" to yourself. Say this a few times. Then ask yourself what you need. Wait for your reply.

9.

THERE ARE PEOPLE WHO WILL UNDERSTAND YOU: PRACTICES FOR HOW TO FIND YOUR PEOPLE

"You know how creative people are; we have to try everything until we find our niche."

—E. A. Bucchianeri

It is true that you must try things before you know where you want to be. We are expected to experiment a little because we are creatives, all of us. Humans are a creative bunch, but society's need for conformity often stifles that creativity.

Finding your people can be challenging if you have been surrounding yourself with people without much thought to whether they resonate with you. You can be deeply connected to your opposite or someone with differing viewpoints. What matters is finding folks who take the time to know you and care about you. Who love you even though you are flawed and sometimes messy.

Your people may be found in very unlikely places. By this, I mean we tend to go to the same places, only talk to people we know, and only engage in familiar activities. Sometimes, we find ourselves gravitating to people who don't really know who we are or folks who might even be problematic for us in the long run. We do this because it is familiar, a comfort zone that becomes so automatic that we have stopped asking ourselves if the comfort zone is serving us or not. Sometimes, we have been part of certain groups for so long that we feel stuck in places we don't belong. Learning to look beyond what we think we know can often lead us to new opportunities and bonding experiences.

It is about making connections that truly matter through commonality, shared experiences, or beliefs. It's just like when you are reading a book, and you love it because you relate to the character or characters in the book. This relational connection is important. If you start attending a group and feel that they are not on the same page as you or are not thinking as you do, go to another group. Go on a quest for people who are processing things like you are, feeling like you are, have ideas similar to yours, and so on. Do not settle. Give your relationships the importance and meaning they deserve. I am not saying be exclusive, but rather be open to finding connections with a variety of folks, and don't put energy into places that aren't nurturing.

We tend to harbor a fear of the general population. We think things like, "What will they think of me? What if someone knows the real me? No one will accept this thought. People will call me unstable." In addition, in modern society, people have lost the ability to care for each other. To be there for each other when things are hard. Instead of supporting one another, we tend to cover up our inability to be there for someone by labeling the hurting person as weird, mentally unstable, or a screw-up. Then we tell them that their actions are unfavorable. When we express our need for help, we are often met with a big red stop sign. Stop being human and go back to being a robot. Can you imagine a world where it was acceptable to be exactly who we are, in all our humanness? It exists. It might be a small group here and there, but it exists. Finding those people is an act of nurturing your soul. Finding those people is an act of self-love. You don't have to fit into places that hurt you emotionally or physically. You deserve a tribe that sees and hears you, even when you are having a hard time. You deserve people who will celebrate with you, grieve with you, pick you up when you need it, carry you when it is necessary, and rejoice with you always. They exist. I promise you.

You probably aren't going to find people exactly like you. That isn't the goal, although it would be great to know someone who feels exactly as you do and believes exactly as you do, but in truth, you probably won't find an exact match. Realize that people aren't perfect. They will come to you with toxic positivity sometimes, but if they can see you and hear you even when they don't understand you, then that is enough sometimes, as long as they are there supporting you. Find people who realize that you have the capacity for mistakes, but you also have the capacity to be present. That is what really matters.

Exercise on Understanding Your Tribe

Ask yourself, "What really matters to me when it comes to relationships? What is important? When I imagine a friend, what characteristics come to mind?"

As well as, "What guiding principles are important to me?" By this, I mean what principles do you honor and feel are important? Examples can be things like truthfulness, trustworthiness, creativity, character, and so on. These principles, which some call virtues, are aspects that shape your community. They guide you. They set the expectations of the group. Consider the guiding principles if you find yourself in a group where you feel you do not fit in. Are their principles in line with yours? Often, they are not. Finding people who value the same things you do is important. Finding people who live their lives by a similar ethics structure helps establish safety because you know the group's rules. You know what is guiding their choices and behaviors. This is a link to more information, a list of common guiding principles, and a website where you can take a quiz to uncover some of your valued virtues: www.viacharacter.org/character-strengths.

10.

PRACTICES FOR DISTRESS TOLERANCE

"Overwhelm is like being sucked up into a dense bank of fog. You can't see your way; it's cold and scary; and you don't know when it will end."

—Me

Distress tolerance refers to a person's ability to handle emotional distress, either actual or perceived. It has to do with someone's ability to be in and work through a stressful situation without making it worse. Your ability to handle situations that arise can profoundly affect your life. Feeling easily overwhelmed can make it challenging to handle daily stressors and nearly impossible to tolerate more serious situations. There are many forms of therapy and alternative practices to help with distress tolerance.

How you handle distress can be partly biological. Your brain, your body chemistry, and the parasympathetic and sympathetic nervous systems (PNS and SNS) all play a role. Your sympathetic nervous system governs what is often referred to as a "fight-or-flight response." Do you run, or do you fight? It can cause increased heart rate, pupil dilation, and production of sweat; it can slow down your digestive system, increase your breath rate, increase levels of adrenaline or noradrenaline secretion, and start the glycogen breakdown system, whereas the parasympathetic nervous system brings you into a state of homeostasis or a more resting state. Here, you are more relaxed; your body can digest food, your heart rate slows, your breathing slows, and you can carry on at a slower pace. All this is to say that your body plays a role in your ability to regulate distress and the emotions that go along with it. However, this isn't all there is to the story; you can develop ways of soothing yourself and regulating your body using various techniques and your mind.

Another factor that can make it hard to regulate distress lies in your memories and history, both your own and ancestral. Past experiences and historical factors influence how you interpret a threat. Long-term trauma, such as violence, war, and extreme poverty, can show up not only in your thoughts and emotions, but also physically, in your body. An example of this might be Post

Traumatic Stress Disorder (PTSD), which is a common response to trauma.

Frequently, people use imagery meditation to help; they might imagine a quiet, safe place, their favorite space, a vacation destination, or something pleasing. People may use a distraction like running or hiking to "get their mind off of it." They might apply Zen practices (being okay with things when they aren't okay) or radical acceptance (just accepting what is and letting go). Physical exercise can help with this as well. Acupuncture, breathwork, meditation, sound therapy, yoga, and aromatherapy can also be helpful, as can a host of therapies, such as Dialectical Behavior Therapy (DBT) and Cognitive Behavioral Therapy (CBT), to name two.

Some of the ways you can get out of your head and the worry that has taken over are through exercise, getting active, doing something that requires you to be present (such as counting repetitions), yoga (which requires you to monitor your breath and practice a sequence), a dance class, or martial arts, which requires concentration.

If exercise isn't your thing, get involved in a group or volunteer. Find something where you can contribute, thus allowing you to express some positive feelings.

Ask yourself, what is the opposite of what I am feeling right now? Once you have figured that out, do something to conjure up those feelings; in other words, redirect your thoughts to something more desirable. Think of something complex but enjoyable, like redesigning your bedroom or remodeling the kitchen. What would you do? Consider every interaction and detail of the project.

When feeling distressed, start a five-minute mindfulness practice. Find a quiet spot, set a timer, close your eyes, and just breathe for a bit. Concentrate on a phrase that will help you and repeat it over and over; it might be something like, "I breathe in happiness, I breathe out fear," or "Let go," a personal mantra that will help you in the moment.

Or apply a technique of naming and recognizing a situation for what it is. Then, acknowledging that it is present in your life right now, look at it and be curious: what are the facets of the problem? What are the components of this issue? Then, normalize it the best you can. Know that you are not the only one with this problem; many people work through it, and you can figure this out. Make a list of things that will help you find one thing you can do right now that will help you feel in control of the situation.

Finding exercises that align with your needs can be a challenge. You may not resonate with some of the exercises I offer in this book today, but perhaps a month from now, they will feel more relevant or doable. When you are in a state of overwhelm or depression, doing anything can be a real struggle. Daily tasks like getting dressed or brushing your teeth become laborious. When you are faced with these feelings, I want you to know that it is okay. It is okay to feel like just brushing your hair is hard work. When this is the space you find yourself in, learn to prioritize your tasks. Start with your basic needs—food, water, shelter, and basic hygiene—and add what you can as you feel your way out of the darkness. Take small steps, and on days when you can run, do that. But know that this path isn't linear. Some days, you feel fine, and other days, you need more. This is true for all of us to varying degrees. We all experience fatigue. It can range from feeling tired, but being able to push through, to feeling so shackled by it that we are unable to move or feel. When the severe appears, realize that you may need to get help. You may need to reach out. Do not become afraid that people won't understand. Fuck them. This is about you. Share your information on doctors, therapists, healers, medications, vitamins, things you do to come out of darkness, and everything you can think of; write it down and share it with someone. Reach out to them when you find yourself sinking too deep. Keep this information handy for yourself. It is you that you are depending on. Use the numbers in the back of this book to find what you need. Call 911 if that is all you can do. I want you to know that you can lean on others in crisis. They will come through for you. The person on the other end of the phone will get you help.

When you need to be alone and when you need to reach for support is a fine line to discern. Have you identified a tipping point for yourself? Have you developed criteria to determine whether you are being alone for the right reasons or just choosing to isolate out of fear of rejection or punishment? Knowing why you want to be alone is key. Develop a list of healthy reasons to be alone because being alone is not a bad thing. It is something everyone needs on occasion, but it is important to know when you are choosing to be alone, and that you are doing so for healthy reasons, such as to work on a project you are doing, to meditate or self-reflect, to write in a journal or read something you are interested in. To take time out from a busy life to rejuvenate and refresh, to do so for spiritual or cultural practices; in short, for a reason that benefits you. Unhealthy reasons might be fearing rejection, fearing punishment, partaking in abusive behaviors, self-mutilation, because you feel people don't understand you, berating yourself with negative self-talk, self-punishment, punishing others, or proving a point—you get the gist. If alone time is a place to obsess about all that is going wrong, or it is used as a place to hide from everything and everyone, that probably isn't healthy. I get it, though; I sometimes have difficulty in social groups. Often, I find it to be an anxiety-laden experience.

It becomes unenjoyable to me sometimes. Knowing when to withdraw or how to manage being out with others is important. Do some self-reflection: do you like to be alone in a crowd, hate crowds in general, or do you want to engage with no more than two people at once? Do you enjoy going to an activity like a movie over an intimate dinner party? That is perfectly fine! Knowing your preferences is really important. It also helps you find your people. Finding others who prefer the same social outings is important. It might be a challenge if you hate crowds and your BFF loves to go to large festivals. You can still be good friends, even BFFs, but you can meet on common ground; perhaps you can go with them to a festival, but you can only handle three hours, not all day. Perhaps they are happy to go to a movie with you next time. Knowing yourself and your needs and being able to express them is vital to happiness.

If you are retreating for reasons that are not healthy—some of which are listed in the previous paragraph, but certainly not all of them—then you are receiving a wake-up call. You are engaging in behaviors that are more damaging than healing. It is hard to change old habits. It is really hard. What is the payoff when you engage in isolation that isn't healthy? Can you get that payoff another way? Do you need to talk to someone about it? If you are engaging in self-isolation for harmful reasons, can you seek help of some kind? If it is too hard to seek help, ask someone close to you to help you find a therapist or healer and call for an appointment and, if needed, help you get to that appointment. It is okay to ask for help. That is one thing I often hear: "If they had only asked me for help, I would have done anything." People want to help you. They do. They might be awkward at it, but it isn't because they don't want to help you. It is because our society has not prepared them to do so. Society has not prepared any of us to handle the hard things. Most of the time, when you experience someone being unhelpful, it is simply because they are not prepared, they lack the skillset, and they don't know how to really help. It isn't because they don't want to. Even if they mask it in anger or blow you off, the deep reason is not the anger or dismissive behavior; it is the fear of not knowing what to do. Not knowing how to be there for someone.

That said, you are worthy of feeling safe. Some people don't know how to provide a safe and nurturing space. It isn't that you don't deserve the space, because you most certainly do. It is because they are not equipped. Either they have not been taught compassion, or they think that compassion comes with limits, or it is weakness. They feel that they don't know how to help. It is a good practice to write down your safe places, where you feel safe, and with whom. When you need safety, you will know where to go and who to contact. Don't keep contacting the unsafe folks hoping it will be different this time. Put yourself first. Who, what, and where do you need right now? Map it out for yourself so you know when you need it. When you are unsure if you need a safe place, seek it out. Don't wait, just go to it. If you are thinking about it, you must need it, so just give it to yourself. You are worthy of safety even when you are unsure if you need it. Learn your warning signs, and when they crop up, seek safety.

What are warning signs? It is hard to know sometimes what your warning signs are. For some it might be uncontrollable anger, self-mutilation, withdrawal, inability to get up and function through your day, anxiety attacks, lack of appetite, lack of enthusiasm for things, quitting doing things you like to do, lack of motivation, talking about suicide, giving up on dreams, giving up on goals, being overly tired or lethargic, losing memory of large chunks of time, abusing drugs or alcohol, abusing others, engaging in risky behavior, mood changes, behavior changes, personality changes and other alterations of your normal behavior, being mean for no reason, yelling at inappropriate times, inappropriate behavior, self-defeating behavior, self-sabotaging behavior, obsessing about things or experiences, abusive and constant negative self-talk, obsessing on death, delusions, hallucinations, uncontrollable outbursts, self-inflicted sickness, feeling foggy or unable to think, physical ailments, lack of hygiene, or severe burnout, just to name a few. We all have warning signs, even those who have never thought about suicide; we all have limits. Learning what yours are and recognizing them when they show up can help you gauge when you need help and when to bring in professionals or healers. Knowing when it is serious and when it is just an ordinary venting session will help you to provide a safe space for yourself. Frequently, these behaviors can lead to unsafe spaces and more destructive behaviors. People may respond to your behavior unfavorably, which can result in you finding yourself in unsafe places or being treated negatively.

Learning to create a safe place for yourself is some of the most critical work you will do for yourself, not just in the moment but throughout life. Safety is a hardwired need. Because safety keeps us alive, it is a biological need. Being able to give yourself safety is essential. Knowing your triggers, warning signs, safe places and people, safe strategies, and ways to protect yourself will provide you with something that you may have never had before: safety within yourself. Resilience and strategic ability. All of which are important to thrive.

At the end of this book, there will be a template for you to fill in all the critical information that you need in case of an emergency. This can be given to a friend when you need help. It is a valuable tool that relieves you from instructing folks or finding information for them when you are in crisis.

"The real difficulty is to overcome how you think about yourself."

—Maya Angelou

11.

COMPASSION PRACTICES: TREADING THE DARK WATERS OF NEGATIVITY TO UNDERSTAND YOUR SOUL

*"You aren't here to be hurt alone.
Don't deny your soul its own awakening."*

—Unknown

Rising above the negative and understanding the soul is challenging at best, some days. Our culture seems to thrive on the misfortunes of others. We are drawn to tragic news, and often catch ourselves wishing for negative consequences to affect someone who has wronged us in some way. It's human. It's okay; you haven't thought anything worse than the rest of us. We also apply these negative outlooks to ourselves. As we have already discussed, we are drawn to negative perspectives. Weeding through negative self-talk and beliefs is a challenge, especially since you often feel that the world is always pointing out your faults. That isn't what is happening, though. You perceive the universe as calling out your faults, but in reality, it is just a thing that happened. The weight we give to things is our own creation. We can decide that a bad test score is a consequence of not being prepared, or we can decide that we are stupid. We are making a judgment call on the things that happen to us and using that judgment to create a response. The judgment is not the truth; it is just our judgment or our thoughts on the situation.

Beyond that, we tend to dwell on the situations, events, and outcomes that didn't go right. We dwell on the mistakes we made, the wrong things we said, the ideas we had that didn't work. We fixate on all the times we just messed up royally. We often find ourselves going over and over an unfortunate event and then worrying over memories of other things we messed up on, too. Pretty soon, we are thinking of the time we were in kindergarten, when we got in trouble for taking the class turtle out of the terrarium without permission. Often, these thoughts overtake our brains at certain times during the night and don't let up until our alarm goes off in the morning. We can obsess about a remark we made that we later overthink into a completely different scenario. Like a bad sitcom episode, instead of just clarifying what you meant to say to the person in question, you obsess about the comment for weeks and start avoiding the person you *think* you offended. The end result is that this episode will be one of the things you think about the next time you are up at three in the morning, worrying about your latest folly. It will take its place in line behind the kindergarten turtle incident. When we do this to ourselves, we are reaffirming negative self-impressions. We are giving our negative self-talk ammunition against us. We are sabotaging our own happiness. We are creating a version of ourselves that we refer to as true even though it isn't. We aren't that person we conjure up at three in the morning. We simply aren't that person at all. We are much more than that. Yet that is the version of self we often think of when we think about who we are. We neglect the other parts, the unsung parts, the gentle, kind, joyful, brave, funny, loyal, intelligent, impressive, beautiful, and glorious parts. We don't think of those parts. We let them lie quietly at our feet without giving them much notice at all. But it is these quiet parts that make up who we truly are.

You will mess up because, my dear, you are a human living a human experience. You will also do extraordinary things because you are so capable of amazing things.

You are a mix of these things. You are not purely good or purely bad; there is no black and white. You will have to live with yourself as a multifaceted jewel of many different things, all coming together to be something complex. You are a tapestry of all things the human experience brings. You will be incredible, and you will have some bad days, you will ride high, and you will struggle, because, dear one, we are all these things. There is no perfect; there are just humans. Humans are complex. You are complex. If you can dip into this notion, you will be given a gift. It's called vulnerability. To realize that you are human, thus vulnerable to mistakes, wrong turns, misinterpretations, and tragedy, but you're also vulnerable to immense joy, happiness, laughter, incredible ideas, and fantastic work. You will have your ups and, I'm not going to lie, your downs. You are going to experience some, maybe extreme, lows. Finding resilience is important, but allow yourself to experience them but not become them. It is okay to move in the space of pain, to be there as you need to, but it isn't your permanent identity. You aren't the kid who lost the class turtle; you are the person who has experienced that and so much more. The complex being who, yes, was perhaps shaped in some way by the turtle incident, but you aren't just that, or any other unpleasant thing that happened. Even if the unpleasant thing is actually a heinous and unthinkable trauma, you may be shaped by it; it will make an imprint, but it is not you. It is something that happened that involved you. It is not meant to be internalized, but it probably is something you will carry with you; some days, you won't think of it at all, and other days, a trigger will bring you back. You will move through this with ebb and flow. There are days when, for no apparent reason, I sob until snot is running down my face, and I have a raging headache as I mourn a loved one who died years ago. There are days when I feel immense guilt over not being with them more, understanding them more, working on the relationship more, and I mourn—oh god, I mourn—that I can't do anything about it now. Some days, these thoughts aren't even on my mind, but appear when a trigger presents itself; it might be a rainy day, a good book, or Folgers coffee with 2 percent milk, and I am there, hovering right next to that suit of grief, so close I could wear it entirely simply by leaning into it. Sometimes, I lean in; this sadness over the loss is weirdly comforting. I will never get over it; I carry it onward, but I also carry all the good things with me. I will carry all the exceptional things that I have experienced. I will carry all the magical and wondrous things, along with heartache, pain, and trauma. It all lives in my soul as a strange and mysterious soup called Juliana. To find your soul in the soup is the key. To carry your pain but not be only your pain. This pain can define your corners but not your entire being. Know that you survived the storm; maybe just barely, but you survived it. You are like an elite warrior: one that is only noticed by those who know what to look for, but you otherwise blend into the surroundings as though you're ordinary.

Exercise

Take a moment to recall a positive memory. Don't give me that; I know you have many, it is just hard to find them as they are hidden underneath all the hard ones right now.

Close your eyes and imagine every detail: how you felt, how it looked, who was there, what time of year, the smell, the love. Think about it in great detail and how it affected you for days, maybe years, afterward. Now, say to yourself, *This is me. This is me, also. I am this, too.*

Do this for a week or more, and think of a positive memory every day. Think about it deeply and repeat that this is yourself: *This is me also, I am this too.*

Repeat until you can hold a happy memory in your heart as easily as you can hold the hurt you are feeling.

12.

THE MYTH OF PERFECTION

"I'm sorry, I can't be perfect..."

—Simple Plan, "Perfect"

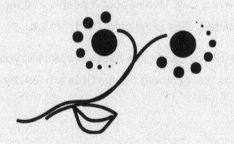

No one is, frankly. Perfect. It is a myth they talk about as though it is a truth, but it isn't. It is some weird ploy to get you to try to be perfect, but honestly, if we concentrated more on being authentic and not on being perfect, we would all be better off. The illusion of perfection creates a serious problem when we are faced with something that isn't perfect about ourselves. Perfection is an unhealthy definition masquerading as something that can be achieved, yet it can't. We can't be perfect, yet society keeps insisting we should be. Like there is something wrong if we aren't perfect when, in actuality, if we were perfect, that would be crazy wrong. It isn't possible. It doesn't exist. You cannot be perfect. I cannot be perfect. Your older brother isn't perfect. That Oscar-winning actor isn't perfect. Human beings are not perfect.

This concept is one of the most damaging concepts out there. We strive to look perfect, with perfect hair, perfect bodies, perfect lips, perfect weight, perfect IQ, perfect SAT scores, valedictorians, best in show, perfect jobs, perfect kids, perfect house, perfect cars, say perfect things, do perfect things, excel at everything, be admired by everyone, be famous, stay perfect forever—but that doesn't exist. As a society, we need to stop wanting this to be a thing. We should demand that the idea of a perfect person be struck from everything we know. It should be something like pigs flying or when hell freezes over, or goonies. It should be a completely ludicrous idea that one uses to explain an outlandish notion.

Can you imagine the energy it would take to be perfect? Or how it would be to have a perfect close friend? Perfection is just too much.

Let it go. It doesn't serve. In fact, the myth of perfection will only hold you back. It will prevent you from trying new things, putting yourself out there, talking to people you want to talk to, making friends, applying to things, stepping out of your comfort zone, learning new things, and basically doing everything fun. If you cling too tightly to the myth of perfection, you will end up being unhappy.

You will become so concerned with what other people think of you that you will self-paralyze. You will stop living for yourself. Living for others is something we easily fall into. We stop knowing who we are, and we become what we think others expect. We become the idea of perfection, at least according to the definition we believe others have. It is just too much. It is unrealistic and unsustainable.

I want you to know something. You are enough. You are enough just as you are. I know what you are thinking; yeah, right, you don't even know me. I may not know you personally, but I know you, and I know you are enough. You are here, you are fighting, and you are showing up to read this book. You, my friend, are enough.

This moment may have you face-down on the mat, but no one is counting you down. Look for the hand reaching out to help you up. They are there. They may not be the hand you want, but there are some who genuinely want to help you up. For one, I would not have written this book if not for you. I am holding my hand out, and so are many other folks. Reach out and take hold of one.

Exercise

Even if you don't have drawing experience, you can do
this exercise. Draw yourself in as much detail as possible.
Draw the landscape around you. Draw any problems
that seem to be ominous; draw your allies, the people,
animals, books, movies, hobbies, and everything that
holds a hand out to you in support. Every time you
think of something—a song that helps you, a poem, a
sunny day, an activity—draw it, walking beside you and
protecting you, shielding you from the problems. You
will probably need a big piece of paper, or you will have
to tape more paper to the initial paper to add everything
that has helped you along the way.

13.

SELF-LOVE IS A PRACTICE: IT IS IMPORTANT TO PRACTICE EVEN WHEN IT SEEMS IMPOSSIBLE

"The most terrifying thing is to accept oneself completely."

—C. G. Jung

Self-love is a lifelong practice. You will fall off the wagon. As soon as something goes wrong, it will waver; it might even die for a while. Self-hatred is often used in capitalistic societies to get you to buy stuff. For example, hate your body? Get a gym membership and buy these supplements. Do you want to find a lover? Make a profile, but use a doctored picture of yourself or even a picture that isn't you at all. Don't tell the truth about your life; make up something that people want. Buy these clothes, and you can't wear the same outfit to the office that you wore last week; people will think you are strange. It never ends. The subliminal messaging from the people who want us to buy their products never tells us we are great just as we are. People who want us to conform tell us our behavior is bad, our thoughts are silly, and our emotions are unwanted. We simply cannot show up as we are; that is unacceptable. We must put on the persona of an acceptable someone, or people will dislike us.

A few months ago, I did an informal study. I came as I am to various circles of folks. I was pretty much my usual self, but I was open about my past. If someone asked me, how was your day? I was like, "Eh, it was hard" if it was hard. Many people were loving and kind, but some were unable to handle deeper conversations. I was told by someone very close to me that just that was not something she wanted to hear. "Why ask me then?" I wondered to myself. I was also told that I could occupy a hard place. But that no one wanted that. Even though they were telling me about their problems, it seemed that my being able to meet them there, in their tough place, was uncomfortable. Which I think means that I can't talk about hard things, even if they come to me with a problem. They aren't looking for me to be open about it. So, what I found in this tiny sample group was interesting. Perhaps some people didn't want to know how you felt when they asked, and they wanted a comforting answer. One that didn't take effort. I learned that they want to tell you their problems, but they aren't interested in honestly discussing them. Perhaps they don't have the capacity to work on their own problems, or they are more rooted in being upset than in change. I offer this observation to say that those experiences with the folks unable to engage crushed me. Some people didn't want to hear about my real feelings. I want to make it clear that I didn't come to them with issues; I simply answered their questions honestly. When they came to me with a problem, I didn't receive it with toxic positivity, but with empathy. I did make one mistake. I should have asked them how they wanted me to help or what they wanted me to do. I tell you this because if I didn't have self-love, I would dwell on the few bad experiences and not be able to enjoy those who were engaged. I would use the challenging conversations to reinforce a feeling of worthlessness. Although I felt crushed by those conversations, it didn't reinforce negative feelings about myself.

Loving yourself is something we all need to be aware of. Take the time each day to check in with yourself. You can so easily slip into self-loathing because we live in a culture that doesn't support positive self-image. Feeling positive about yourself does not make others money. If you feel bad about yourself at work, then great! You will not expect to be paid more, or you will never feel secure, so it is easier to make you do things at work, because somewhere in your brain, you don't feel secure at work. We have fallen prey to societal conditioning. It is up to each of us to overcome this within ourselves. Small compassion practices like the ones offered in this book and others you can find online can be very helpful.

Some of us are more at home thinking we are not worthy than we are feeling good about ourselves. We are comfortable feeling bad about who we are. We know how to do that. We might even think that we don't have to try hard at anything or that we are incapable of doing things well. This stops us from trying anything. If we do something that society thinks is inappropriate or even heinous, we use this as a way to self-punish. The act of self-punishing includes not allowing our inner dialogue to be kind or compassionate and using names to describe ourselves like stupid, ugly, deviant, trouble, criminal, bully, let-down, and so on. We live in a space of our wrongdoing, never moving through it. If we did something mean in middle school, we let our disgust for that moment become our viewpoint of ourselves, even if we went on to do kind and compassionate things. We don't give ourselves the ability to grow and change. Some of us feel that we are innately flawed and that there is no hope for us. We create a self-fulfilling prophecy that we spend our lives living up to.

Forgiving yourself is important here. We all make mistakes, we all fall down, and you are not alone. Finding forgiveness for yourself is important. Maybe you circle back to the person you bullied in grade school with a heartfelt apology and a place of understanding. Perhaps they still hate you. Then, you look to forgive yourself. You are not that same ten-year-old child; you are older and wiser, and you can decide that you made a mistake. It wasn't cool, but you can forgive your child self and find compassion for yourself. Ask yourself, "Did I do the best I could with what I knew at the time?" It is easy to look back on mistakes with hindsight. We forget that we did not possess hindsight at the moment of the mistake. At the moment, we were doing the best we knew how to do with what we had. I imagine it must be really hard to forgive yourself for egregious acts. I can't say I have any experience with that, although we all have different versions of egregiousness. If this is you, seek help with this issue. Maybe you can't move through it alone. It's okay. We all need help in this life. It is impossible to do it all alone.

14.

HONORING YOURSELF, YOUR BOUNDARIES, AND YOUR OWN CARE

"When we fail to set boundaries and hold people accountable, we feel used and mistreated."

—Brené Brown

Part of loving yourself is about honoring yourself and your dignity. It isn't about seeing yourself as perfect, only looking for accomplishments, or pushing yourself beyond your boundaries to be a high achiever. It isn't about achievements, awards, kudos, accomplishments, or anything else. It isn't that you can't feel good about them, but they are just a tiny fragment of who you are. They are part of your tapestry. The true golden threads in your tapestry are how you honor all the parts of yourself. Making a mistake and working through it allows the sadness to have a place at the table and allows you to appreciate the stories it tells when it comes to visit. It is about welcoming the things that aren't so great and providing yourself love and support as you work through those things. Part of that support is knowing when to pull back and take care of yourself. It is unconditional because it does not mean you condone your bad behavior but that you find grace for yourself. It is the ability to support yourself, to listen to your inner wisdom, and to love all that you are, even the things you consider to be flawed.

Honoring yourself through a self-love model can help you better understand your boundaries. Boundaries won't magically present themselves to you. They are complex. Often, we let a societal expectation or boundary override a personal boundary. For example, some people end up engaging in unsafe behavior as a consequence of trying to uphold a societal expectation or boundary.

When you feel like you need to stay home and rest and drink tea in bed, but you also feel obligated to go to a company party—this is an example of boundary conflict that we all must navigate. Do you honor your feelings, or do you go to the party because you are trying to get a promotion? Do you go to the party for an hour and then cut out early to enjoy some quiet time? If you are unsure, tap into your inner knowing. Because somewhere inside you,

you do know. You know what you need, but frequently, we find ourselves caught between what we want and what others expect. This is somewhat natural in society. We all must do things that we don't want to do or that aren't fun, like doing laundry. It isn't an enjoyable task to most, but it is an act of self-care. Just as a caregiver would do your laundry when you were little. I am not talking about these acts of give and take in life. I am talking about boundaries that honor the self. What are your boundaries around self-preservation, self-love, and self-care? For example, what are your boundaries around dating, relationships, personal time, money, career, goals, etc.?

Figuring this out is complicated and requires flexibility. The boundaries you had around friendships at thirteen may be different from relationships in your thirties. Being flexible on boundaries allows you to grow your boundaries as you grow. It gives you the freedom to evolve and adapt as you learn.

Having boundaries about your own care is important. We all heal and grow in different ways and respond to different modalities. Sometimes, someone's best intentions can be more damaging than if they remain silent. Establishing boundaries in the realm of what you need for your support team is necessary because, frankly, they are as lost as you. They are unsure how to help you. Giving them guidelines is helpful. Having guidelines for yourself is also beneficial. It is easy to spin out when you are so overwhelmed that you have lost a sense of what you need. Boundaries or guidelines help you navigate when you are overwhelmed or exhausted. They help you understand what you need and when you don't need something.

One note about boundaries. Sometimes, when you are in a state of crisis, people who care about you may have to cross them. You may say that you want to be alone at a time when it probably isn't the best thing for you. Sometimes, when you are in the deepest part of the forest, you are unsure what you need; someone else may make those decisions for you. That is when you add grace to the mix. Allow another to help you. Boundaries should not be so rigid that you cannot make adjustments or compromises when situations are dire. Remember, just because you let a boundary soften in time of need, that doesn't mean you can't firm it up the next day. You can. You can be flexible. Of course, some boundaries can be more rigid. Boundaries that are deeply rooted in beliefs or virtues may be more rigid, but others should have enough flexibility to allow for help when needed. Of course, I am not talking about applying this concept to all boundaries all the time. For example, if someone wants to have sex with you and you don't want to, that can be a rigid boundary. If you don't do drugs and someone wants you to, that can be a hard boundary. If you value loyalty and someone asks you to do something shady to your best friend, the boundary can be more rigid.

You can honor your boundaries and find space for understanding. Sometimes, we talk about boundaries as something that must be a rigid wall that we protect fiercely in our lives. I get that. Some boundaries are sacred; others are more fluid. We all have different boundaries for different people, too, which may change over time. The boundaries I have for my dentist are different from the boundaries I have for my partner. Some are different; some are universal. Understanding your various types of boundaries can be very helpful in navigating relationships and our role therein.

Discover what boundaries are more rigid than others within yourself.

Boundary Exploration Exercise

Make a list of your boundaries. This list is flexible; you
will subtract and adjust them as needed, so let this be
a flow exercise; just write down what comes to mind.
Categorize them if needed, such as boundaries for sex
and relationships, boundaries for friendships, family, etc.
Now, which of these are most rigid? Why are they rigid
for you? Write it down. Is it rigid because of a core belief
you have or a virtue you admire? Is it rigid because of
the consequences that occur? Pull out the boundaries
that might be important during a health crisis. Make a
separate list for those and add it to a packet you are
going to create for a person who may be helping you
navigate a health crisis.

15.

YOUR REALITY IS YOUR INVENTION

"We see what we believe, not the other way around."

—Seth

To an extent, this is true. How you see the world is your reality. If you choose to see a person hurting or in pain rather than an asshole holding up the line at the mini-mart, in doing so, you tend to feel compassion rather than anger. If you see an issue you are having as an obstacle to figure out rather than an unsolvable problem that you can't fix, it might be easier to overcome. If you view obstacles as horrible things you can't work through, you create a reality of anger and helplessness. This is not necessarily a truth, but you create the framework, the lens through which you see everything and decide on everything.

If you see everyone who cuts you off in traffic, or is driving in a way of which you don't approve, as jerks, and you get mad at everything that happens, then your reality will be one of people trying to take advantage of you. You may even think that the world is against you. If you see the same conditions as just someone having a bad day or other drivers being late to something important and small incidents as just part of life, you tend to be a more compassionate and calm person.

In all these scenarios, you start to look for confirmation of your beliefs and emotions by pointing out and noticing other things that confirm a belief. What I mean is, you look for more of the same, and you tend to put more energy into the things that prove your theory and belief and overlook things that point to another theory. You notice what confirms your beliefs on reality more than what opposes that view.

Suppose you are unsure of yourself or you are fighting for legitimacy and belonging in a relationship. In that case, you may find yourself being hyper-critical or judging in an attempt to point out your worth. This will create a reality of "me against you" instead of thinking of your relationship in terms of "us" and "we."

You begin to separate yourself from everyone else, and you close yourself off to the dignity of others.

When you are fighting for equality, to be seen and heard, valued, and appreciated in a relationship, and you become fixated on those inequalities, you blind yourself to what is working. I am not saying you should stay in the relationship, but I am saying that your reality becomes one of a horrible relationship, and you must hate the other rather than feeling like, *This isn't working out for me; I am not getting what I want. Do I want to compromise because other things are good in the relationship, or is the weight of what is not working tipping the scales?* People who can successfully determine that may realize that, while the other person may have had good qualities, it just wasn't balanced enough to remain in the relationship. Others may burn bridges.

How you relate to and see the world directly correlates to how you relate to and see yourself. If you think people are innately evil, does that mean you are innately evil? If you judge everyone else's work harshly, does that mean your work is being judged harshly? Maybe so, but also, maybe not. These ideas are just thoughts; they are not the truth. You don't know if they are true or not; all thoughts are just perspectives.

Have you ever walked into a room and felt an oppressive or bad vibe and immediately felt sad, mad, or unhappy? Have you ever been at a party, and someone walks in, and you can't help looking over at them? The energy you put out to the world affects what you get back. If your energy is oppressive, people will avoid you, or you may find yourself in unsatisfactory situations more often. If you are positive in nature, your outlook on things is more forgiving and understanding; you might find yourself enjoying things more. Where one person sees a car going through a red light and thinks the driver must be a jerk, other people may see the same thing and think it was a haggard person who wasn't paying attention; they might even add the thought, *I've been there too*. And feel a bit of compassion.

I am not telling you to be all rose-colored glasses with everything that happens in life, but notice how you see the world. Is it serving you? Is it helpful? Do you need to be more balanced in life? Sure, be leery of walking down a dark street at one in the morning in an unfamiliar part of town, keep yourself safe, and be realistic, but also check in with your thoughts and make sure you are balanced.

People often say, "If you think you can't, you can't," and "Life is what you make it." These sayings refer to your inner mindset and how it shapes your reality. Your mindset can stop you from achieving your goals and dreams and having the life you want. It can also lead you down the road that takes you to incredible places. Working on having confidence in yourself is huge when it comes to personal success. Success is different for everyone— and I am not talking about the success you think you should have because it is an expectation of society, parents, or partners and such, but your definition of success. Feeling self-assured and having a positive mindset go a long way to help you achieve the things you want to achieve.

Cultivate more positive thoughts about yourself and the world around you. Work on changing your inner dialogue when it is self-deprecating, self-defeating, or naysaying. Allow yourself the freedom to dream. Allow yourself the trust and confidence in who you are to shine through the negative talk in your mind. Check in with yourself often and ask yourself, "Is this a negative belief that no longer serves me? If so, what other beliefs can I have about this situation?"

Remember, a thought is just a thought. It is not the truth. I often think of this when people talk about spirituality and which religion is true and correct. If believing in a particular dogma or religion helps you get through life, then it is true for you. If I want to believe that I have a spirit guide helping me navigate life and that belief helps me and improves my life, then it is true for me. The absolute of everything is about belief. Belief makes things real. Real is personal. You don't have to convince others of it or prove it to be true.

If you wholeheartedly believe in something, then it becomes a truth for you. Be mindful of what you choose to believe, because that shapes your reality. This means that you should not hold onto beliefs that hurt you (negative beliefs about yourself, for example). Keep beliefs that help you (you are worthy, for example).

16.

REGRETS AND THE POWER OF "I AM SORRY"

"Never forget the nine most important words of any family: I love you. You are beautiful. Please forgive me."

—H. Jackson Brown Jr.

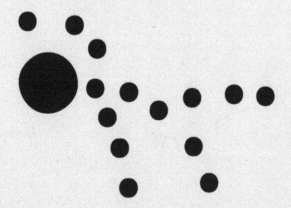

Regrets. We all have them. Most of us can trace our regrets back to our earliest memories, back to our own beginnings. How we relate to our regrets fertilizes what we cultivate. Seeing regrets as failings cultivates self-hatred, low self-esteem, and even shame. Seeing them as tools to go deeper can be the life-giving water to understanding, compassion, and inner love. In addition, they color all the feelings in between. Having a regret means you can empathize with others. To feel a pain you caused as though it were your own. It can mean that, through hindsight, you see that your choice may not have been the best, but that you can benefit from it anyway. Regrets are little lessons about how to be in the world and who we want to be in the world.

Some people stifle regret with justification. I am sure you know these folks; they are never wrong. How do you feel about them? I am guessing, not so good. Regrets sit in the lap of vulnerability. Vulnerability allows you to see the regret and to understand your role in it. People who justify it probably find it too painful to be vulnerable. They may have had a few horrible situations happen when they tried to be vulnerable, and now, they hide behind justification. They are off-balance when it comes to vulnerability because it is scary to be vulnerable. Our society does not think of being open as powerful. Society believes that, in order to be powerful, we must always be right.

Same with crying, which is an outward act of vulnerability. You are showing the world that things matter. Something touched you in such a profound way that you reacted with a physical action. Your mind and body know. But how many times have you heard, "Don't cry, it isn't what someone like you does," or "Crying is for babies"? If that were true, we would have lost the ability to cry as soon as we got out of diapers. Crying is actually a strength. It takes guts to cry in these times. It takes guts and bravery to be authentic. To announce that you are a human being with emotions, and you hurt when others hurt. You are connected to everyone and everything around you, and that is nature, that is real, that is bravery!

This brings me to saying sorry. Saying sorry and putting the actions behind the behavior. There is nothing more trite than an insincere "sorry" told to you with a sneer or a strange voice. Also, "Sorry, but..." My daughter taught me this one, and you know, she is fucking right. Just be sorry if you are sorry; once you add a "but" to the conversation, you are saying that you aren't truly sorry. Find another language. Be sorry, that's the end of the story. Then, put your money where your mouth is and put action behind the words. "Sorry" has immense power when it is real. It can bridge even the most significant divide. Sure, there may always be a different way of reacting to each other after "sorry" has worked its power, but there will also be acceptance. People will feel as validated as they possibly can in the moment.

Some people won't accept a genuine apology because they perceive it as not genuine. You can't do much about the reality other folks are conjuring up for themselves. You can only work on your side. Being genuinely and sincerely sorry allows you to work through the issue, and it fosters dignity.

17.

FINDING BALANCE WITH EXTREME TRAGEDY (WHAT IS HAPPENING IN THE WORLD)

*"I don't think of all the misery,
but of all the beauty that remains."*

—Anne Frank

Recently, I stopped watching the news. I still look at my news feed, but I don't spend hours scrolling and watching clips of stories I am interested in—mostly because I realized the stories I gravitated to were not uplifting, but tragic. When I saw something tragic, I felt so much sympathy and always felt like I had to do something about it. I started to speculate on what the future would hold. It became very stressful. I didn't know how to get out of the cycle of emotions and dread. Over time, I kept retraumatizing myself with new stories. They would haunt my thoughts so often that I felt that the world was blowing up.

Many of us are drawn to all the terrible things going on in the world. It might be because we are sensitive and emotionally available. We immediately sympathize with the suffering of others. Because of this, we take action. We turn the stories of suffering into action rather than using them as trauma inducers. Some of us are very interested in social justice and have taken on the much-needed work of improving life for all bodies. Some of us either are part of a group or have loved ones in a group that is persecuted, marginalized, and devalued. We feel deeply for those suffering, and we feel a calling to help where we can. Before we go further, let me say thank you. I appreciate your work and dedication. Empaths and sensitives are also at risk of absorbing the suffering of others. These groups of folks bear the extra burden of societal expectations that they will fix things. Empaths feel the need to absorb pain, activists feel the need to change things, and sensitive people feel the need to listen to every hard story and be a sounding board. It can be too much. It is vital to keep a balance (that word again) between the work that you are doing and the beauty that exists beyond your work.

There are good things here on Earth, too. Sometimes, it is hard to remember that. When you are so deep in the suffering that exists, you often forget to occasionally rest your eyes on something else.

We can also feel extra sensitive to the trauma of others if it triggers our own trauma experiences. We subconsciously look for connection, even if it is to connect with survivors of tsunamis or refugees from war; we see ourselves in their suffering, and we can have immense empathy for them. We don't want others to suffer as we have. Layering our own trauma over tragedy stories can make everything seem too much to bear.

If we find ourselves in a work or life situation that is causing burnout or extreme fatigue, we can become more prone to seeking out stories of suffering; in doing so, we can become obsessed with their suffering. In a way, the trauma of others helps us normalize our own issues, even if they are not of the same magnitude. We find ourselves becoming over-involved in the emotions of the situation. We let the tragedy that is out there become our definition of life.

Some of us become over-concentrated on tragic stories around the world as a way to understand the reasoning or the why. What would people kill other people for? Why is this happening? Why are we creating an us-vs-them situation when we should band together? We simply cannot understand it, and in order to rectify our understanding, we process it constantly. I remember doing this when the Columbine shooting happened. I felt like my heart was torn apart. I ached for the other caregivers, friends, and community. I felt deep sadness that there are people who think their only way out of their suffering is to kill others. I felt for everyone: the victims, the survivors, the caregivers, the teachers, the community, the rest of us affected by the suffering, and even the boys who decided to gun down people they knew. Heartbreaking. I was glued to the news and any stories there were. I talked about it, and I cried for them. I was devastated. How has humanity come to this? Our systems for help, recovery, and grief are so very broken; how did we get here? How can we change it? It seemed a hopeless situation for humanity. It was a turning point for me. I must be brave enough to say something when I think things are broken, to grieve even for people I will never know. It wasn't a complete takeover and hijacking of my emotions, and it did allow me to make this turn, but there were moments when I could not see the good things all around me. Caring neighbors, a fun and excited daughter, a wonderful family, a community of creative folks, friends, lovers, good memories, sunshine, nature, and candy. For a brief moment, I could only see suffering.

If you think I am talking about you, then learning to balance suffering and beauty is important. It is important to celebrate the good things, the victories and accomplishments, the wonderful things that happen, and the people who are doing amazing things out there.

A few things you can do to limit your intake of emotional factors associated with suffering might be limiting your news intake and engaging with positive storylines in your entertainment (books, movies, music, TV, social media, etc.). Make time to decompress with activities like exercise, breathwork, meditation, self-care, yoga, and anything that takes your mind off the suffering for a bit. Do not start speculating and/or obsessing about the future, using negative themes to create a future in your mind that contains even more suffering.

Volunteer or be part of things that make a difference in the realm that brings you so much emotional unrest. I was living with my daughter and partner in Ventura, CA, when the Thomas fire happened. The fire burned for weeks; you merely had to look out your window toward the burned-out neighborhoods to see the devastation. Fire trucks were everywhere, the smoke was so harmful and dense that you couldn't go outside, and ash was everywhere. People had died, people were missing, animals were missing, animals were gone, lives were gone, people were traumatized. There were people we knew who had vanished. Neighborhoods that had been evacuated were now ghost towns. I had to drive through the actual fire to get to work. The fear that I might die commuting to work. The fear about who would care for my daughter if I died—I could taste it on my lips, and it coated my throat with fear. "Did I tell her I loved her before I left?" went through my mind each day I got in the car. The salty taste of death is still vivid and real all around us.

My daughter and I were alone, without power, not knowing when or if we would have to leave our home, cat cages and essential papers sitting by the front door in case evacuation had to be quick. It was a lot. Many of the now homeless and evacuated animals were brought to the fairgrounds, where people were asked to bring food and anything else they could donate. The fairground was over its animal capacity, but the pets kept coming and had to be driven to neighboring areas. We went to every open grocery store, bought food for cats and dogs, and delivered it to the check-in stations. We bought food for people too. We did this a few days in a row. We began waving and honking at the firefighters and thanking them when we saw them at the store or sitting and resting on their trucks. We grieved with them when the fire took one of their own. We honored them in every way we could. Helping others gave us purpose, a moment to feel relief. Shopping for dogs and cats and people we would never know. Thanking firefighters, buying random folks' coffee, and just coming together as a community to help one another.

It is undoubtedly compassionate and appropriate to realize that there is suffering, tremendous and deep suffering, in the world, both far away and in your own household. Finding a way to grieve and balance your emotions is needed for your personal harmony.

It allows you to be there for others, both in their joy and in their sorrow. Happiness allows you a place to rest and rejuvenate. Joy is part of the human experience, and being joyful and appreciative will enable you to spread more of that energy out to others. How many times have you been in a bad mood, and a cute dog or cat made you smile, and you forgot about being grumpy even for a second? That is why cute animal videos exist; they are a place where we can take a moment to rest and experience a little happiness. They shelter us from the suffering. It is nurturing to your soul to both give and receive mutual understanding and joy. You can be like a cute animal video to others once in a while by giving them a place to rest in joy, even if it is just a smile to a stranger or an understanding nod to a parent wrangling a toddler into a car seat. Spreading loving awareness is as important as any other work you will do.

In a way, Anne Frank outlines one of the concepts of mindfulness: to think of beauty and spread love even when you are experiencing extreme hardship and fear. It is important to find a corner of your mind that can feel something positive. Dwell there in equal measure. If you are having a hard time, force yourself to be in nature, notice the beauty around you, watch a fun movie, or do some self-care.

Exercise on Balance

This exercise is on finding gratitude. You have probably heard of gratitude journals. I urge you to keep one in whatever form works for you. Some people use pen and paper, others have a private Instagram account where they take images and write down why they are thankful for what they saw, others record their gratitude, and others say them in meditation. There are many ways to practice daily gratitude. Find one that works for you and work with it daily. What are you truly grateful for and why? When you need to, look back and reflect on what you are thankful for. Allow the joy of knowing, having, and experiencing these things to be present within you.

18.

RESILIENCE IS A SUPERPOWER

"If your heart is broken, make art with the pieces."

—Shane Koyczan,
Blueprint for a Breakthrough (2013)

I absolutely love this quote. It reminds me that there are so many ways to look at something and, in that ability, to bend and be flexible. In doing so, we become resilient.

No doubt, the word "resilience" has been used in the form of toxic positivity, maybe toward you and your situation: "Get over it," "Be more resilient," "Stop obsessing," and so on. But people rarely know how to help you be resilient.

For some people, the roots of resilience lie in a spiritual practice. The feeling that there is a divine order to things that helps them understand. Others view hard times as life lessons, a way of becoming more than they were yesterday. People who value compassion feel that hard times give you a more remarkable ability to love freely. Many people apply mindfulness practices, such as being in the moment and being okay with what is not okay. To be able to say to yourself, *I wouldn't say I like the situation, but I am okay with it nonetheless*. This was me when I was contemplating suicide. I was reading a Zen book, and it clicked. I had been grappling with the concept of being okay when things weren't okay and one day, it clicked. I can absolutely hate the situation I am in (the feeling, the people, the lack of compassion, the loneliness, the devastation, the loss, the grief, the inability to grieve, the inability to "just get over it," the shame, the deep, deep sadness), but at the same time, I can be okay with it. I could be okay with this uncomfortable space. Once I got that, I shifted. A lifelong practice of mindfulness became my road to resilience. Things still hurt. Some things will take a lifetime to overcome (if it's even possible). I bend to the wind and know the storm will be over soon, but at the moment, I bend and endure the wind, rain, and sheer cold. Inside, I know that the storm will bring the flowers.

Letting go can be the foundation of resilience for others. Letting go but still learning and moving through challenges is a superpower. Not just letting go, but understanding the reasons and even lessons in a painful situation, can be very enlightening as you move through life. It can be crucial for some to work with the belief that all things happen to provide growth. To approach a problem to know more, to be more, to live more. It is part of your purpose. I can genuinely say that I would not be writing this book if life had not given me the experiences I needed to come to you as I am. It is the compassion and empathy I developed during hard times that allows me to feel the love I have for you. I felt a calling to reach out. None of this would have been possible without the things I have endured and lived through.

For others, resilience is becoming closed off to any uncomfortable things. These folks may be called "emotionally unavailable," or mean or uncaring, or distant or loners. They may be people who surround themselves with friends but never let the relationships go too deep. The ones who make sarcastic, mean jokes without realizing they are hurtful. The people who don't remember things others say unless it involves them. They are often self-absorbed and unable to connect deeply. I don't recommend this practice. It isn't really resilience. Resilience is about weathering things and moving through them with your emotions and thoughts intact, about enduring something and living in the richness of the moment. If you close yourself or parts of yourself off to the world and others, both now and in the future, you are reacting to a situation, and fear is most likely at the wheel. The fear of getting hurt, being laughed at, being misunderstood, being found out, being unloved. Fear has its place in the context of a living creature. Fear keeps us safe, but it also knows no boundaries. If you let it regulate your life in a way that is too confining, then fear becomes an unsafe factor.

Resilience is a superpower. It is the ability to have things blow through you and around you without breaking you. You can take on a storm knowing you have the tools to get through it. You don't end up constricting yourself, but opening yourself up to more. Resilience gives you another perspective. You may come to realize you need a boundary where you didn't have one before. This may happen because you came to know yourself and your needs a little more intimately than you did pre-crisis. You may never "get over" what happened, not in the sense that modern society wants you to. You will be different, but you will also be okay with the difference. It will hurt some days, my god, and it will hurt some days, even years later. Resilience isn't forgetting; it is remembering and living with the scars. It is in seeing scars as beauty marks rather than grotesque features that the magic is found. In that space, the lessons reveal themselves to you. This is another factor in how you define your reality. Your reality and resilience are partners. Resilience is dependent on your perspective on a situation. If you approach a problem with thoughts that are defeating, if you carry your defeats with you as though they are a rigid definition of who you are, it will be hard to be resilient. This mindset does not foster a perception of things in a way that allows for growth. You are perceiving things in a way that supports your negative self-definition. The important thing about resilience is realizing that your perspectives are crucial to your ability to move through things with a resilient outcome.

Consider an issue you are having. Make it something less devastating for now. You can work up to more significant situations over time, but be good to yourself and pick something manageable. What is the issue? How are you approaching it? Do you feel defeated, like it will never change? Do you think you are incapable of fixing it? Is it too much to bear? What perspectives and self-image definers are you using to develop these thoughts? Do you think you are stupid, powerless, not brave, etc.?

Now consider different perspectives: What if you had a positive perspective? How would you approach this issue? What if you were brave (or any other positive traits that you don't think you possess)? What are different ways you might approach it?

Are you willing to try one of these perspective changes for your problem? Remember, people tend to want you to stay the same, even if they criticize you and your beliefs; they tend to continue to want you to be the person familiar to them. Their idea of you is a comfort zone of sorts. If you veer out of that comfort zone, they get confused. But don't worry, they will shift. I want you to be aware that there may be resistance, but hold true to yourself. You are brave, intelligent, and capable. You can shift into a space of resilience, and it will be a good thing.

19.

—

BECOMING INCREDIBLE

"To be yourself in a world that is constantly trying to make you something else is the greatest accomplishment."

—Ralph Waldo Emerson

Okay, this was a teaser. I felt that you might be intrigued, especially if you think you are not so incredible. But my friend, you most certainly already are. This is about living into your power, knowing within your quiet self that you possess magic and that all things are possible if you think they are. This is about owning your worth.

This isn't about ego, thinking you're hot shit or anything. This isn't about being an attention-grabber, seeking a spotlight, or having it your way or the highway. That isn't power, that is simply using manipulation to get what you want. I am talking about Beyonce's power. I am talking about knowing who you are, accepting who you are, everything that you are, even the hard parts. This is about finding yourself and loving that person with wild abandon.

How is this done? I mean, it is pretty hard work. Just when we think we have mastered it, someone comes by and says something that makes us feel weak and unsure. That is the work. To figure out who you are. When you know who you are, you learn to hear the hard things and still stay true to yourself. This doesn't mean you disregard what people say; it means you reflect and respond to what people say to you, or when things happen, you let it in and reflect. That you allow yourself to either shift or decide the information was not helpful. Sometimes, people say cruel stuff just to feel better about themselves. These comments can be released immediately; that is an "it's not you, it's me" scenario. Those folks have their own things to work on.

Becoming incredible is a byproduct of working on positive internal dialog, changing perspectives that hold you back, working on self-love, finding gratitude, being compassionate, and tapping into your wisdom within. It is also a byproduct of self-acceptance, vulnerability, and love. I know that sounds corny, but sometimes the truth is corny. When people call things corny or dorky, they are just uncomfortable with the truth it holds. They are playing an us-vs-them game.

Here is a shortcut to being the person you want to be. Just start being that person. Think the way that person would think if old doubt creeps in; tell it to leave. Start listening, start caring, and start doing what you want to do to find your purpose. Start, just start. Of course, you will have days when things are challenging. Remember, recovery is not linear, as is any path in life. We are creatures of curiosity; we will veer off a path to look at meadows or a vista. We will want to retreat to something we know. We will seek comfort in things that may not be as comfortable as we think. It is all part of being incredible. It is often said that the most interesting people in life are the ones with the most wrong turns. Consider this life a grand adventure. It's incredible, just like you are, but if you keep it locked in a cage in the dark, you will never see just how wonderful life is and you are.

Exercise on Finding Your True Self

What is your dream self? List it out, draw it out, and work with it until you get to a place that seems right. Consider factors of this dream self as goals and other factors as things you already possess. What can you do to move toward these? What one thing can you do today to work toward that self? Write down at least fifteen things you already are that are in sync with your true self.

20.

YOU HAVE SOMETHING VALUABLE TO CONTRIBUTE

"Never think that what you have to offer is insignificant. There will always be someone out there that needs what you must give."

—Anonymous

I cannot tell you how much your unique perspective contributes to all of us. Just by being here, in your suffering, you are showing all of us that we, too, have the bravery to show up even when it is painful and hard and it feels hopeless. You are here! You are here. It is important.

As you know from the statistics around suicide, there are a lot of bodies out there who are feeling hopeless. Who is hurting? There are people you know who may not be so involved in your life right now, but years from now, your example of living through the darkness will have a profound effect on their future life.

You are contributing in other ways, too. You are not all just this pain you have now. You have contributed and continue to contribute to life and the lives of others in small ways, from helping a kid tie a shoe to smiling at someone walking down the street. You have no idea how profound small acts of kindness can be for people. Sometimes, no joke, a smile from a stranger can keep someone going another day. A few hours ago, a woman called me to talk about her mother's death. She went through a bunch of details about her family statistics. She didn't speak much about her feelings for her mother or her grief; she talked about where they lived, what year they went to this school, and that restaurant they used to go to for lunch. She recounted where her doctor was, what street her mom's friends lived on, and the car they drove. It was a conversation where she spoke, and I listened. In the end, she genuinely thanked me for simply listening. It was then that the voice cracked. She needed to tell someone of her mom's legacy, that her mom had mattered in this community. Her mom's kindness to people at the deli, how she babysat neighbors' kids, made cakes, picked up groceries, and drove people to doctor's appointments, mattered. She was right, it mattered to the receivers of her kindness. It mattered.

This life is an interwoven tapestry of small moments that are all significant to the pattern we are weaving. The little things we do and think nothing of are significant to others, although we may never know.

Do you know someone who needs some kindness? We all do. It was silly even to ask. Acts of kindness help us find meaning in our lives. Helping others is very fulfilling, but many times, you help people without even realizing it.

This exercise is simple; practice at least three acts of simple kindness each day. Maybe it is opening a door for someone, letting someone with a few items go in front of you in line, or hugging a friend who needs it. Practice mindfulness by contributing every day.

21.

UNDERSTANDING WISDOM

"The source of all-knowing is in you."

—Eckhart Tolle

Eckhart Tolle says it all here. You know the way. You know
the path. You are the healing you seek. Tapping into believing
in yourself and how you feel is challenging, though. We are
continually barraged with information. How to be, how to act,
what to do in this situation or that, how to talk to people, how to
be more influential at work, how to act on a date, and everything
else you can think of. If that were not enough, then there is all of
the subliminal messaging that indirectly tells us about all of the
societal expectations or desired characteristics that "valuable"
people need to possess. With all of this messaging coming at us all
the time, it is easy to forget how to believe in ourselves and trust
our instincts. We find ourselves constantly critiquing ourselves
with hyper-critical eyes. This is different from self-reflecting. I
am talking about your inner critic that tears you down and makes
you question your own beliefs and thoughts. Self-reflecting is
an exercise of a completely different nature. In the upcoming
chapters there are a few tools you can use to foster and bring
out your inner trust and wisdom. It will lead you to ways you can
better tap into your inner knowing and to feel secure in who you
are and what you think.

22.

FINDING SELF-LOVE

*"You owe yourself the love that you so freely give
to other people."*

—Anonymous

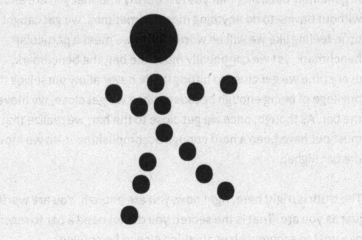

Okay, so we have talked a lot about self-love already. I know it is hard to give it to yourself, especially when you feel that you are unworthy. That is the key. Feeling worthy will lead you to self-love. It has been my personal experience that, no matter how many books you read on the subject or terms you have learned about self-love, it is not the same as feeling self-love. The information has to make its way out of your head as a thing you read and into your heart as a thing that you are. I am talking about internalizing this knowledge. Not just using the information to understand the concepts of self-love, but living into it as a way of being. As a practice.

Feeling into this knowledge is essential to finding true self-love. I like to call it letting the knowledge trickle down from your mind into your body, into your heart and soul. Until it becomes part of you, it is only knowledge that you have. I feel that some of this lies in genuinely believing that you are worthy and that you are enough without having to do anything more. Sometimes, we get caught up in feeling like we will be worthy once we meet a particular benchmark, yet we continually move the bar, the benchmark, every time we get close to hitting it. We never allow ourselves the privilege of being enough because, when we get close, we move the bar. As though, once we get close to the bar, we realize that it must not have been a hard enough accomplishment, so we move the bar higher.

The truth is, right here, right now, you are enough. You are worthy just as you are. That is the secret: you do not need a bar to reach or a goal to accomplish or anything else to be enough.

You are always enough. Being enough isn't part of the growth you are thinking will bring you worth. They are two different things. Personal growth is growth, maturity, understanding, development, deeper understanding, deeper knowledge, more ability, greater peace, gentle nature, compassion, and so on. Being worthy and having worth is something you are born with. You are worthy regardless of your past, your trauma, your mistakes, your challenges. You may achieve great things, obtain dreams, and go on to surprise even yourself, but it will not bring you any more worth than you have right now. Because right now, my friend, you have an abundance of worth.

It isn't egotistical or self-centered, or self-absorbed, or conceded, or loudmouth. None of these things are about self-worth. On the contrary, they are about lack of worth. They are outward expressions, a cry, a plea from the unconscious knowing to be validated. These are acts one does to get external validation from others. It is not self-worth, but lack of self-worth, that creates these qualities of someone's personality.

Being unworthy is not an act of humility. I thought this for a long time, but that is false, too. Humility is not putting yourself down or devaluing who you are and your contributions. It is not about dying in a gauntlet of shame and guilt. Humility is about surrender. It is surrendering to the inner knowing that all people are worthy. It is surrendering to the loving awareness that we all possess. Humility is doing great things but not feeling the need to be validated, because you have self-worth; external validation is not a requirement. It is unnecessary to prove your worth because you already know you are worthy. Humility is quiet; it is an internal smile; it is warmth that tends the fires of your soul.

Once you live into your worthiness, you can take the next stepping stone, which is self-love. Self-love is knowing that you are who you are, that you love deeply into all that you are with grace, understanding, and compassion, and that you forgive yourself fully. You learn from life as it happens, both the wonderful and the hard. You embrace all the parts of yourself with love. You do not have to approve of some of the things you have done, but you love yourself regardless. The two are not connected. Forgiveness for yourself is the bridge between the things you may have done and self-love. Forgive yourself; you did the best you could with what you knew at the time.

If you do something that you regret and you can't fix it, it doesn't make you unlovable; it makes you human. It is a human experience. Your mission is to ask yourself why. Why is it here? Why did this present itself? It isn't to be internalized as a lifelong punishment. It isn't to show you that you are a terrible person. It isn't there to reinforce something horrible someone said to you. It isn't part of your worth; it is part of your human experience. What you do with it is the real work.

Things happen, terrible things; thoughts come to mind, horrible thoughts. No one is immune to these possibilities. We all experience them, even the rich and famous. You only have to Google "famous people losing everything or royally fucking up" to see a long laundry list of trials and tribulations, some of which could be defined as heinous. It is human. It is not about your worth. It is not about their worth. It is about being human, because no matter how much fame and money you have, you are, in the end, living a human experience.

Here is something I found helpful. It is important to let go of things that used to define you in order to let new ideas emerge. For example, I always defined myself as an abuse survivor, which I am, without any thought to how that plays out in my world. Over time, I generated a lot of fear around men and situations that stopped me from living a full life. I can be a survivor, but I don't have to let that definition define how I should act in the world.

Conversely, how I act is not necessarily a definition of self. For example, if I define myself as not being smart, then I will never be secure in what I know. If I define myself as an uncaring jerk, then it will be hard for me to be openly caring because I may feel people will think that is out of character or I might be embarrassed. If I define myself as a very nervous speaker, then I am closing the door to being able to give a great public talk because that action is in direct conflict with how I view myself. If I am using a past trauma to define myself, then I am closing the door to just being happy. Think carefully about the self-definitions you have. Are they really who you are or just a trait you have due to circumstances? Is having a belief that you are a shy person stopping you from being spontaneous or trying out for a community play, even though you want to? Our self-definitions are parameters we place on ourselves to conform to a belief that, guess what, is just a belief, not a truth. We feel strange going against these beliefs because they conflict with our self-definition. We worry about what others will think if we just show up as someone else. I get that! I let, and continue to allow, shyness to be a self-definition, and it stops me from being truly who I want to be.

Find Your Worth and Let It Show You Your Love

What are you worthy of? To make a list, it must fill a page and have at least twenty things on it. Start each sentence with "I am worthy of..."

Make another list using the same parameters as the I-am-worthy-of list, but start with, "I love myself because..."

What experiences can you let go? Make a list. Start each sentence with "I am worthy and _____ does not define me."

Put the list of what you are worthy of somewhere where you can look at it daily and repeat each sentence aloud. For the second list of what you are letting go of, cut each item into a separate small strip of paper. Each sentence should now be on a small strip of paper cut from the list.

Find a ceremonial bowl or vessel. You may have to go in search of this, or you may already have one in mind. Your bowl should be able to hold a burning object. Incense burners or candle holders can work well if they are big enough.

Take your first strip of paper and read it aloud: "I am worthy, and _____ does not define me." Then, put it in your bowl, thank it for the lesson, and set it on fire. Do this practice safely, and make sure you will not catch anything else on fire. If fire isn't an option, use water. Tear the strips into small pieces and soak them until they are pulp and the ink washes from the page. Go through all your paper strips this way, and take your time. At the end, say, "I let go of everything that does not serve. Thank you for giving me the gift of a human experience."

Do this as many times as you need. You may use the same items until you feel you have completely let them go, or you can do new items as they come up.

23.

EXPERIENCING BOTH THE SCARY AND THE BEAUTIFUL

"The wound is the place where the light enters you."

—Rumi

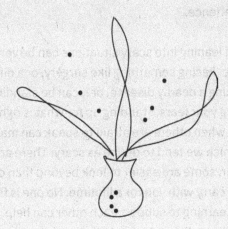

As you have probably heard already, we would not understand the good without having experienced the bad. That is, the definition of good is intertwined with bad. They cannot be separated.

The scary is scary because you have decided that it is based on past experiences and experiences of what isn't scary; what isn't scary is already known to you. What is scary is often unknown. We can't define it and map it out and guide it as we want to, so therefore, it is scary. We have also decided that scary is bad. Why? Some people thrive on the thrill of what scares them. How is that possible? It is their mindset that they choose to decide that scary is thrilling. Scary is worth it. Scary pushes you beyond your current boundaries and into a new place. Again, as with everything I say, I am not speaking about extreme danger or anything like that; I am talking about the unknowns we face in life. The times we step out of our comfort zones and try something new. The times we decide that being a newbie is better than never trying at all. The times we take a chance on something scary. It can be a pretty life-changing experience.

Observing and leaning into scary situations can be very uncomfortable. Facing something like surgery, or a difficult treatment, facing a deadly disease, or it can be standing up for yourself, facing your fears, standing up for what is right, or being the lone voice when others are afraid to speak can make you feel vulnerable, which we tend to define as scary. There are many degrees of fear; some are easier to look beyond than others. Some fears you may carry with you for a lifetime. No one is free from scary things. Learning to support each other can help. Have the hard conversations, listen deeply to the hard conversations, help someone, be there for someone, support someone. All of these things are needed by us as a collective. To see when someone is genuinely afraid or terrified and to help them through it. Is someone helping you? Is their help helping or hurting you? If help is hurting you, then consider guiding your helper in a way that is more useful. Frequently, we want to help, but we don't know how. Our society isn't so good at teaching people how to support each other.

The point is that scary things usually happen because they make us feel vulnerable. Being vulnerable is not a bad thing in itself, but you must be brave enough to stand in that space. It is scary to be open, unprotected, and unsure. Knowing when to be genuinely scared to take care of yourself is, of course, something you need to pay attention to. You don't have to take unwise risks (that isn't what I am talking about); in fact, that is something else. Allowing yourself to be vulnerable is an act of compassion. By being vulnerable, you allow others to be the same. Vulnerability is bravery.

You are worthy of the beautiful things and of enjoying them. They are all around you all the time. Sometimes, we think that we must be in a beautiful place and travel to somewhere special to see beauty, but that isn't the case. Wherever you are right now, look around. Can you identify anything of beauty? Maybe you have an outfit you like, or you see a color you like, or whatever; beauty appears everywhere in physical form. From a misty vista at sunrise to the pleasing logo on your coffee cup, beauty is abundant. It is all there in physical representation. Beauty is also present all around, in the unseen: a good memory, a great idea, good vibes, good moods, the scenarios you create in your mind in the form of positive daydreams, meditation, good music, anything that touches your soul that makes you feel hopeful or happy or positive.

You are also the creator of beauty. You can also be the creator of fear. Understand your power and understand that it is not about wielding your power, but about using it in ways that build up rather than tear down. We all hold the responsibility to create a world we want to see. Choose wisely.

Practice Noticing Beauty

Give some thought to the beauty you put out there in the world, from the doodle on your notebook that time when you were bored, to the time you helped someone who needed it. You have contributed so much beauty over your lifetime. Feel into your beauty. Lean into something good here. You don't always have to lean into the hard things.

24.

GRATITUDE FOR ALL THAT IS WONDERFUL AND IS HONORING YOU

"Gratitude is the closest thing to beauty manifested in an emotion."

—Mindy Kaling

Your job here is to pay homage to all that you are thankful for. All your reasons to live, your spaces of comfort, your joys and beautiful sorrows, your dreams, your desires, your loves, your obsessions, your generous heart, open and exposed. Lay it all on the line. Leave it all on the page to be taken in by your own eyes. Become drunk with the notion that the wonderful is honoring you. It has arrived, and it is always by your side.

Go ahead, write them down, take pages to do so, be thoughtful, be lighthearted, be introspective, mystical, woo-woo, rational, outlandish, reserved, and in the end, smile shyly to yourself because you got a lot! I offer a few to get you going:

- Good conversations
- The touch of another
- Creating what you imagine
- Music
- Art
- Stories
- The love of a good pet
- Perfect moments
- New things
- Old things you love
- Good food
- Good drinks
- Great friends
- Lovers old and new and yet to be
- Sweetness
- The soft morning air
- A hard rain
- Snow when it isn't expected
- A day off
- Another day off
- Road trips
- Traveling
- Staying at home
- Coffee
- Tea
- Slurpees
- Laughter
- Good books
- Movies
- Popcorn
- Clean sheets
- Someone else doing the laundry

- A quiet moment
- Loud moments
- Parties
- Staying home
- Free concert tickets
- Discovering new bands
- Book stores
- The ocean
- Trees
- Flowers
- Mountains
- Being limitless
- You
- Me
- Us
- Memories that sustain rather than hurt
- The beauty and serenity in nature
- Someone who really understands me
- Feeling pure joy and happiness
- Kindness, giving, and receiving
- Seeing something that takes your breath away (in a good way)
- Being amazed by the unexpected
- Helping others
- Belonging
- The seasons
- Moments of bliss

I could go on, but it is time for you to write your own list. Prepare to spend some time, because the list is endless. You can stop when you feel it's good enough, but know that it will always be incomplete. There will always be more. Some of the things on the list you have yet to know, some things you know but need to be reminded of, and some things you used to dislike but now enjoy (like broccoli).

Also, examine where you find value. What is meaningful to you? What are the things in life that make you feel connected to others, to nature, to something more collective, to the universe? What are the things that give you a sense of wonder? What is beautiful? What is your meaning to life? You can know this within yourself. That joy is there. Uncover it.

25.

HELPING OTHERS, VOLUNTEERING, FEELING COMPASSION

*"The best way to find yourself is to lose yourself
in the service of others."*

—Mahatma Gandhi

Helping others gives you purpose, value, and connection. In helping others, you connect to them on a deeper level. This is part of living in a community with others.

In an individualistic society, like the one we have here in the US, we lose sight of the bigger meaning of humanity. That primal need to be connected, needed, valued, appreciated, and part of something can go unfulfilled. We often find our internal voices telling us to be greedy and jealous and not wish for the success of others. Somewhere along the way, we were led to believe that the success of others is at the expense of our own. This is untrue. This is a teaching from a money-making perspective: don't let others get your share of the pie. People go so far as to sabotage others. We also neglect each other as a form of punishment. We don't value the young or the elderly. Everyone is fighting for value. At work, we fight against each other for raises and promotions, we jockey at PTA meetings over whose child is the best, and we judge others by their looks so we can feel better about our own. We can find ourselves in a pretty hostile space if we don't balance it with compassion. When you volunteer or help others, you expose yourself to a different kind of community. One that needs your help and one that gives freely. Finding the pocket of comfort here is enriching. When you connect with folks who volunteer, you tap into a group of folks who care. Volunteers are the nurturers. Many come to this work because they know what it is like to be neglected in some way. They have a desire to give what they may have never received themselves.

Mutual aid is a movement we should bring back. Rather than competing, we should be trying to lift each other up. It can take a lot of work to find pockets of this occurring. In my professional life, I often found myself in places that were governed by hostility. People hated the students, the staff, the faculty, the parents, the regents, the president, and everyone in between. There were uncrossable boundaries and a severe lack of sincere kindness and care filtering down from the deans' offices and alike. The message was to get in line and be quiet. One individualistic person with power and a lack of understanding of the human aspects of their work can poison an entire branch of a company. People may never see their role in the deconstruction. They may not see how stifling their lack of compassion is to positive morale and work environment. Climbing the corporate ladder becomes the only thing they see. In essence, they are climbing the ladder while stepping on a lot of heads. Some people have gotten off-balance, becoming more self-serving than other-serving.

Serving others is not so hard. Consider causes you are interested in and become involved. If one organization isn't your vibe, seek another until you find a fit. Volunteer without a big commitment; maybe you can participate in a beach cleanup when the mood strikes. If you are going to commit without having a set schedule at an organization, make sure you make a point of connecting with others so that you can start integrating into the community.

You would be surprised at the places that have volunteers. For example, a local venue may use volunteer ushers. If you like music or theater, consider that option. You don't have to be limited to nonprofits. You can volunteer to visit people in the hospital or elderly folks in assisted living facilities; you can be a baseball coach and so much more. Take a step in the direction of a connection and see where the road leads.

26.

SELF-CARE PRACTICES

"Self-care is more than the basics; it is a sacred ritual of love used in the celebration of your soul."

—Anonymous

Being good to yourself is part of self-love. It is an honoring of who you are to the core of your existence. When you engage in self-care, you feed the soul and tend to the vessel that houses your being. It can also be an escape from the harshness of the outside world. It can be a place to rest and rejuvenate. Like spending time in nature, my favorite of all self-care rituals. Communing with nature is an important ritual for the senses. Whether it is a vigorous hike or sitting quietly on a rock, nature is a powerful healer. Don't underestimate her powers. Try to fit nature into your self-care, even if it is to look out your window to see the maple tree change colors in fall or feel the crunch of frosted grass under your boot in the early morning. Some believe that spending five minutes barefoot walking in nature (no sidewalk or human-made materials under your feet) is skin-to-skin contact with the great Mother Earth. For example, when you were a kid, you played barefoot outside. Try it out; immerse yourself in a simple walk on a natural surface.

For all other self-care techniques, of which there are an infinite number, they all embody the same thing: a ritual that celebrates your self-love. They are important.

To be honest, I once did a podcast saying that I didn't understand self-care. I leave it up on my channel to remind me of how far I have come and how I possess the possibility of change and growth. Sometimes, a reminder is needed. After all, as humans, we often forget to care for ourselves.

Breathwork can be a really lovely and free self-care practice. It isn't for everyone, but it can help you to reset and relax. The practice can be as simple as breathing in deeply and slowly for the count of four, holding your breath for the count of four, releasing your breath slowly for the count of six, and repeating at least ten more times. This simple exercise has been proven to slow your heart rate and help your body recalibrate to an equilibrium state. Even just taking a deep breath before you speak to someone can make a huge difference in how you relate to them. It can help you to hear them more neutrally or to pick your words wisely when needed.

There are many types of breathing exercises. You can imagine breathing through your heart and out through your heart. You can breathe in love and breathe out what no longer serves; you can breathe in thinking, "I am calm," and breathe out, "I am safe," and all kinds of work. Breathing exercises have been used to work with trauma and anxiety, too. Sometimes, breathwork is very helpful to do right before bed, because it allows you to relax before sleep and helps alleviate the stress you may be feeling. It can also help with nightmares and other late-night thoughts that may have become part of your sleep routine.

27.

NATURE AS HEALER

"Look deep into nature, and then you will understand everything better."

—Albert Einstein

Consider nature the mother of all there is. The gentle soul that feeds you, bathes you, and cradles you in her arms when sleep is elusive. Let the mother smooth back your hair and brush your tears away. A simple walk on a tree-lined street will do.

There is no getting around our primal need for the natural world. There is a longing living deep within us that calls out to nature. It is said that the ocean is a mirror to your soul and that we are drawn to the sea because of that. The forest provides so many examples of living through extreme conditions and surviving. A tree hit by lightning sprouts up new shoots from the roots, which are still alive. A tree uprooted and thrown hundreds of feet in a tornado manages to sprout a new branch, which eventually becomes another tree. Even grass gets mowed, eaten, walked on, and starved of water but still manages to grow, reseed, and come back with vigor. Anyone who has ever tried to rid their yard of morning glory or ivy knows the perseverance and determination of nature. Even though we choke it with pollution, nature adapts. When a species goes extinct, another rises to fill the gap. Nature as a whole has a resilience that we are simply not aware of.

Nature also knows the true power of ebb and flow. Through the tides, the seasons, the sunlight, storms, and life cycles, she shows us the divine power of pause. Sometimes, a pause, a moment, is the difference between a successful crop and a failed one. Learning to pause and take a step back before you move forward can solve a lot of issues. It is simple. Without the pause, an ebb, there would be no flow. Staying in a state of flow, of enjoyable movement, is one of life's magical experiences. You feel it when you lose track of time creating or working on a project. You feel it in a great conversation, an amazing book you read from cover to cover in a day, listening to music and realizing hours have gone by, being at an event where everything comes together, being with someone who gets you. Flow shows up in life in many ways and in many forms. Sometimes you do not realize you are in a state of flow until you are out of it. The flow needs the ebb to pause and reflect.

Nature constantly shows us the pleasing quality of symmetry. Symmetry can be found anywhere, from a cell in your body to a massive redwood tree. Symmetry creates balance and harmony. When you feel life is getting off-kilter, find the symmetry of nature, the petals of a flower, a succulent that grows in a spiral, the stripes on a zebra. Although we are not actively aware that we do so, humans often consider symmetry in their definition of beauty. Many people are unsettled when an art piece isn't centered, or something in their house isn't centered to their liking. We seek balance in our lives even if we aren't aware of it.

When you can spend time in nature and observe it deeply, take time to appreciate and be grateful for nature. Dig in the dirt if you can. Buy and care for a houseplant. If that is too much, try some cut flowers. Revel in the power of nature and the beauty of harmony. Rest in the arms of nature.

28.

EMOTIONAL RELEASES

*"Emotions must come to the surface to release
the past that binds."*

—Dana Dason

Don't underestimate emotional releases, but be mindful of how you go about them. Emotional dumping on someone and displacing anger are probably not the best options.

In the book *The Smell of Rain on Dust* by Martín Prechtel, the author discusses the practice of grieving to the ocean. Part of the ritual is telling the ocean all the stories, songs, and sorrows of your heart over the loss of a loved one. Saying your grievances and sadness to the wind, to a body of water, to a tree, or anything in nature can be a massive release. It is an incredible release, just to say it aloud. Writing in a journal is also helpful.

Exercise can also be a way to get your entire body involved in the process of releasing. I cannot tell you how many times I went on a long run and cried through most of it, releasing bad experiences with both my emotions and my body. I imagine a kickboxing class could be very cathartic!

Being creative is another way to release stuck emotions. Leaving it all on the canvas or paper or whatever media you use. Being able to express feelings in a way that isn't through language can be very powerful for both the artist and the viewers.

Music is an amazing tool for release. Many people create playlists based on moods. Just allowing yourself to commune with the music of someone who is feeling the same can be profoundly healing. It reminds you that you aren't alone and that others, even famous musicians, know how you feel and have been there.

Finding a place to talk about your feelings can be incredibly healing, but as we have talked about before, many people are just not equipped to hear someone else's unhappiness. We need to get better at this as a society.

Animal companionship can be very powerful in finding space to let go. An animal friend can help you through rough times simply by showing you loyalty, friendship, and love. Petting an animal can be soothing.

Dr. Deepak Chopra, author and world-renowned spiritual leader, has a seven-step exercise for emotional release that involves meditative practice. He argues that we should allow ourselves to think deeply about an upsetting event or situation and observe it as though it is a movie playing in front of us. He goes on to elaborate on attaching a name to your emotion, such as "fear." Do you feel unappreciated or unloved? Name it. Then let your awareness drift to your body; where does the emotion show up in your body, and what does it feel like? Once you have identified where the pain is showing up in your body, you say to yourself, "It hurts here." Then, the process goes on to taking responsibility for the memory and feelings attached to the memory, not in the form of guilt but realizing that your response to the situation, the emotion, and the feelings are a response you had to the situation, not the actual event. Release the pain through breath and understanding; talk and be open about it. Doing this diffuses the power the event has on you.

Suffice it to say that there are many rituals for emotional release. There are many different therapies and techniques that you can use to work on emotional release. If therapy isn't an option, there is a lot you can do on your own.

29.

ONLY YOU CAN BE ON YOUR LIFE JOURNEY

*"A ship is always safe at the shore,
but that is not what it is built for."*

—Albert Einstein

Please don't forget that you have infinite potential. Your possibilities are limitless, and you can redefine this journey at any time. Ever since I was very young, I wanted to be a writer, but I lacked the confidence to do so. I am a mildly dyslexic person who was in school before this was a thing people got helped with. In my time, I was classified as a bad speller, someone who couldn't even get the shapes of letters and numbers straight. I was given extra homework, and people assumed I was not paying attention in class. I was also someone who didn't understand the directions of right and left. I spent way too long working at other jobs that were unfulfilling and, frankly, sad. That is, until I decided to go for it. To try to achieve my dream. By this time, I was old, an old lady. I changed the course of my life. I am not unique. Many people do this. The hardest part is believing that it is possible. You can be, become, evolve into, or do anything that brings you happiness. I know you can because I was once someone who thought they could not. I was once hopeless. I will never know exactly how you feel because each person is unique, but I know that what is possible is infinite. Know that you hold the unique key to your potential, and you alone are the only one who can open that door. Know that what is behind the door is of your own making.

Someone once told me that your dreams will come true, but there may be twists. You might want to be a novelist, but you are good at short stories; don't devalue the talent you have. Being a writer takes many forms. What they meant was don't be rigid; allow for flow, allow for the current to take you in new directions, and see if it brings you joy. Maybe it brings you the knowledge you need to achieve a dream, or to a person who will help you, or who knows! The point is that this is a journey, and a lot can happen. Adventuring toward our tomorrow is exciting! There might be rain along the way, so bring a jacket and boots and know that, as much as there is rain, there is warm, delightful sunshine and calming breezes. In between this weather, infinite gradients of other types

of weather will present themselves. Meet them all with a fresh
perspective and an open heart.

If you need help, find a partner to help you along your journey. A
friend, mentor, or family member who is willing to journey on with
you. Transformational coaches, therapists, spiritual guides, and
so many more modalities are at your feet, waiting to be utilized.
They can be found by conventional methods, but if you are unable
to engage in these methods, you can find a wealth of knowledge
on YouTube, Meet Up, and other social platforms.

Part III

FOR PEOPLE SUPPORTING A PERSON CONTEMPLATING SUICIDE

"When you don't have the strength to take another step, ask those you love to pull you."

—Unknown

I want to make it clear: you are in uncharted territory. Our society just hasn't prepared us for this, but that doesn't mean we can't do it. We can. You can. Thank you for being brave enough to support and help another human. Thank you for putting love before everything. Thank you for being open, understanding, and present for someone in need. We need more of that. We need to find ways to support each other.

If the isolation brought on by the COVID-19 epidemic taught us one thing, it is that we need each other. We need to have a support system. We heal better with love. Isolation is not an answer; it may keep us safe for a while, but it won't enrich our lives as much as our connection to others will. It is hard to support people when there is no roadmap, when the vistas are unknown, and when you don't know where to find the next gas station. But it can be done. It is done every day by people like you. You can do this. I know it is hard to imagine, but this moment will also have one of those doors we discussed earlier. Don't try to fix this with rigid ideas or closed minds. Come to this space with open arms, acceptance, and a dedication to collaboration. Come to this space knowing that whatever feelings may be expressed, they are real and important. Know that deep listening is itself part of the healing. Know that this is not a place where you have all the answers; it is a space where you help others find the answers for themselves. This is not a space to enforce the law; this is a space to connect on a level so intimate that it will be uncharted, and that is okay. You are right where you should be; be open to what comes.

Bearing witness to the pain of another can be triggering. We all come to the circle with our own experiences and traumas. We come with our own ways of dealing with things, with our own opinions and judgment, rules, and beliefs. There are some things we must put down if we genuinely want to help another person move through hard things. The skill is found in knowing when to lead and when to support—learning from the person who is in the depths of the darkness. You will need to listen deeply and respond with care. You will learn when to be gentle and when to be firm. If a word or phrase is not appreciated, stop saying it and ask for words that work or would be appreciated. You are an ally here; you can make mistakes, and you will make mistakes, but you must also learn how to support in a way that works for the person you are supporting. Learn when to do what. It is very delicate, and there is no set pattern or steps for you to follow. What is important is to be open and compassionate and to let your inner knowing help you through this. You do not have to be a rock for the other person, but you can be a soft place to rest or a safe harbor. Feeling your way through the darkness is scary but also necessary.

As you move through this part of the book. I urge you to read the first half if you haven't already. Although this section concentrates on supporting another person, it is important to understand everything that comes before this chapter.

In the following chapters I offer you a few points of understanding and concepts to lean on. There are many ways to help someone. Use your inner wisdom, your intuition, and your knowledge of the person you are supporting to guide you. Do not lose sight of your compassion, even when it is hard to hold onto; when you are angry as hell at them, remember to pause. Take a breath, and check in with yourself; what do you need? Are you safe? Do you need support? Is this too much, or is it manageable? Ask yourself, "Am I balanced, or have I gotten off-track?" Throughout this process, checking in with yourself and asking yourself these questions will help you to stay in a place where you can offer help and support. It is crucial that you remain anchored to the shore, so that both of you don't get lost at sea.

Here are some guides for you. Remember, there are many
thoughts on these topics, and I urge you to be a seeker of
information. Add things to your toolkit from multiple sources.
This is a strategic and loving act you are entering, and you cannot
be strategic if you have blinders on. You cannot create lasting
change with a rigid and stiff model. That will only cover up the
problem, which will be unearthed another day. It will not create a
shift. To shift, you must be open to all the tools that are there for
you. If you want to truly help, open your mind wide, stretch it to
the edges of all that is known, and then go beyond. You will need
more than one source of knowledge to fight this battle. This battle
can only be fought if you unite with each other. You aren't fighting
each other; you are fighting a common enemy. Together. It isn't
about you fighting them or you being the source of all knowing.
It is about you guiding, supporting, listening deeply, responding
with loving awareness, reacting when needed, and standing side
by side on the battlefield, knowing you have each other's backs
when the going gets tough. It is about considering all things as
you develop a battle plan and shifting when needed. Rigidity will
not win this war; it will only cause problems. Be open. Be wise.
Be understanding. Be compassionate. Be what you can, and bring
in reinforcements when you need to; this isn't a failure, but a
battle cry. You are fighting dragons, sometimes many of them. An
army may be required. You will be surprised at how many people
will join your fight. Remember, you are not alone either. Many
have fought this battle, many are still fighting, and many have
just begun.

1.

WHAT IS A CRISIS VS A SCARY, DIFFICULT, OR UNCOMFORTABLE CONVERSATION?

"People rarely change without first feeling understood."

—Douglas Stone, *Difficult Conversations*

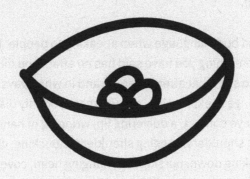

What someone experiences as a crisis may be different than your definition of a crisis. We often put the other in our shoes, meaning we think their crisis is silly or no big deal, so we disregard their feelings. Children who have suicidal thoughts might be thinking their life is over because a friend moved away or a pet died. Their crisis might be something you think is easy to get over, but for them, it is a massive mountain, the top of which they can't even see because it is so far away.

Often, people who are experiencing a bad breakup irritate their friends because the friends think the person should "just get over it already."

The point is it doesn't matter what you think they should think. It matters what they believe and how they feel. Helping them through life's downs allows them to work through it. Not acknowledging a crisis for someone actually creates stuckness, shame, and anger. If our moments of crisis are not acknowledged, we may stuff them down, internalize them, or make them more significant than they are. These experiences may become part of our self-definition and create self-loathing and shame. We may tend to bury it deep down, not realizing that a heavy rain will unearth it once again. A crisis will keep coming back until it is addressed.

Learn to read body language when speaking to people. Learn to see when something you have said has an effect you didn't mean it to. Learn to see what affects people and in what ways. Learn to notice a change in expression, a smile that suddenly disappears, a change in eye contact, a quivering lip, wringing of hands, shrugging of shoulders, sagging shoulders, slouching, change of posture, looking down, pursing lips, hanging head, covering part of their face, trembling, leg twitches, and so on. Learn to read when something positive can be seen in the body language of another and learn the language when things hit wrong. This will serve you not only in hard conversations but throughout life. The body often says more than the words.

I want to talk a little bit here about toxic positivity. We often use this method as a seemingly helpful alternative to listening deeply to someone and attempting to understand. We say things like, "Don't worry, you are young, you will find someone else," "You'll make another friend," or "Things will be better tomorrow." All these phrases seem like something you'd say to cheer someone up, and at times, they may be the right thing to say. Still, if you are using these phrases to get out of dealing with the hard conversations or to circumvent real issues, then such seemingly positive statements become toxic to the person hearing them. Toxic positivity is often used by people who believe a positive spin should be applied to tragic situations and crisis. It is our discomfort with emotions at play here. When you apply this method, you give the directive that the suffering person just needs to just stop and be happy even if they aren't. You are saying that the person's pain and distress aren't valid. But they are very valid. Putting on a happy face isn't the answer. A smile should be genuine, not fabricated because your sadness or grief is not acceptable. We all engage in toxic positivity sometimes. We all want our loved ones to be happy, but sometimes, we need to go to the hard places before we talk about the rosy days ahead. Sometimes, we just need to give someone space to move through their process. This doesn't mean ignoring them until they are happy again. This means being there for the grieving part and being there for the dark days. It is in finding understanding and knowing when positivity should start finding a place in the conversation.

Do not use positivity to cover up emotions you are uneasy with. Although you may think that helping someone in crisis is a lesson that the other person is learning, it isn't. You are learning, too. You are learning how to support someone, what a crisis is, understanding, compassion, genuinely being there for someone, listening, hearing, being silent, being open, pausing, not internalizing, realizing the roles you may have played, shifting, becoming, growing. This process is a learning experience for everyone involved. Do not let your ego tell you otherwise. You will have to be a guide; a guide needs authority at times, but it is done through grace. It isn't a tale about who is smarter but a tale about being human together.

Believe people. Practice trusting that people, in general, are doing the best they can from moment to moment, and at times, people's best may not be accessible for many reasons. What I mean by this is that people cannot always be what you want them to be, particularly if emotional, physical, and cognitive abilities are hindered by grief, sadness, despair, deep shame, unhealthy habits, and a whole host of other factors. People may not be able to be functional. Going to a family dinner and engaging in cheery banter may not be accessible to someone, even if, in the past, they were the life of the party. High work performance might not be accessible if even reading an email is too much. Believe people when they tell you what they can and can't do and when they confide in you. Do not use toxic positivity by saying something like, "Oh honey, that isn't that bad," or launching into a story about yourself. Listen, and respond with a gesture of compassion if it seems appropriate. Instead of launching into advice mode, ask, "What can I do to help you?" Adopt *a what do you need from me* approach and then believe them. Don't second-guess them. Many people adopt the belief that if someone is in crisis, they are somehow a five-year-old who needs direction and discipline. That is not what people need. The truth is that they may be so deep in crisis that getting dressed is extremely laborious, but that has nothing to do with their intelligence. Just because someone is in crisis, that does not mean that they can't think or are being deviant, or liars, or have no idea what they are saying. That is a throwback to the "hysterical woman" campaign that was used to keep women out of the workforce and politics. We now use this historical model for anyone who isn't presenting as a successful robot of society. Hear this, people: people in crisis are smart, understanding, incredible humans who are simply human. To openly be human in a society that doesn't accept the hard parts of life is incredibly brave and smart. They realize that, in the unshackling of the human spirit, they are allowing you and everyone else a space to be human. What a fucking gift! So, stop treating them like babies with no knowledge, and see them as the incredible human being that they are. Praise their ability to be vulnerable by bowing to it in the form of equality. Because, listen, you may find yourself in crisis one day. And the beautiful being that you are helping is helping you to understand human crisis.

If you want to push an agenda, perhaps it is therapy. Be collaborative first. Do not act like the person in crisis isn't capable of their own choices. Ask them about their needs, outline them, and ask them about their goals. Ask them how much capacity they have. All the help in the world will not do anything if the person can't receive it. Get a sense of what they can receive. Don't force someone to a modality that might not be in keeping with their beliefs. In other words, if they work things out through somatic practices or with a mind-body connection, don't force them into a therapy they don't resonate with. Coach them into areas they may not have considered, but don't think they need you to push them into places. That will not be successful. Instead, coach them to the modalities, programs, or therapies that might serve them but, ultimately, give them the power to create their own healing. It is that power that allows a person to move through the darkness. Being dragged along the path by someone, however well-intentioned, will not create long-lasting healing. Giving someone the tools to use the next time around is important. If a person gets pulled along, they have no ownership of their healing. Without ownership, they will lack the tools needed to find healing the next time. They will continue to face the same dragons over and over again until they can create a different outcome.

Here are some simple coaching questions that may help you. Ask the person what they want to do. How do they feel about this or that? What resolutions do they want? What are the motivators for them? What first steps are possible for them? What goals do they have? And so on. Keep the questions about what they think, how they feel, what they think will help, how they see the road back to health. Come to them with understanding, even if they say something that is against your personal beliefs. Listen and ask them how they want to go about things. It doesn't mean you can't take the lead in a crisis, but work on trust and understanding first if possible. If you have a plan that both of you worked out ahead of time and you must take the lead, you are honoring the person in crisis, and that is very powerful. Having a game plan for a crisis is very helpful; we will discuss this later.

2.

SUPPORTING SOMEONE THROUGH A MENTAL HEALTH CRISIS

*"In every crisis, doubt or confusion,
take the higher path—the path of compassion,
courage, understanding and love."*

—Amit Ray

As they say during the safety presentation on a plane flight, you must secure your oxygen mask before you help the person next to you. You must make sure you are safe, able, and willing to take on this work. Ask yourself what capacity you have. Is this relationship a priority, or can you only help in small doses? If you can't be fully present due to your own issues or even past trauma, how can you create a community to help? Consider your gauges for capacity level. When will you know you need to pause, or rest, or withdraw for a minute? What signs will tell you? Maybe it is down to emotions; maybe it is an emotional or physical response to the person in crisis. Maybe it is that you only have the capacity for a daily check-in and then a longer conversation one day a week. Maybe you are all in, whatever it takes, but remember, you also have basic needs, such as sleep, food, rest, etc. How will you handle your mental capacities? How will you make sure you stay well? What do you need? Maybe you also need your own support. Get that in place. Have a conversation with your support team about what they can handle. What do they have the capacity for? Rally community, whatever that means to you: the person's friends, other family members, other people around you who have been through similar things, health professionals, people who work with folks in crisis using different modalities, your practice for health—what is it? It is time to stop being individualistic and lean into community. Of course, do not let go of anything told to you in confidence. Collaborate with the person you are trying to help.

Also, know you will make mistakes. You will. Things may get heated. How will you handle this? What will you do? If possible, work all of this out for yourself beforehand. Try to solve for things you think might come up. It's not that you must follow a script to a tee, but what will you do when you take a wrong turn? What will you do during an argument or if an argument leaves you feeling bad about what you said? Can you circle back with understanding for both yourself and the other person?

I have to tell you that communication is desperately needed here. Be the best communicator you can be. Don't belabor everything, but also use the phrase, "I am sorry" freely. Say, "Thank you for telling me." "How can I help?" "I made a mistake." Do not fail to be human; come to this knowing you are only human. There is only so much you can do, and you will struggle sometimes, but you are here. You are helping. That is more than most folks feel comfortable doing.

I talk to many families who say they knew something was going on, but they ignored the signs, they pretended it didn't happen, they applied toxic positivity, they used band-aids to help keep it all together, and they regretted it. The regret is stifling at times.

So again, thank you for being here, for taking action, and for caring enough to be vulnerable and open.

3.
—

RECOVERING AFTER A CRISIS

"Recovery is not about being right;
it's about allowing ourselves to be who we are
and accepting others as they are."

—Melody Beattie

Recovering is actually uncovering what was underneath all the shit life piled on top of you or someone you love. This section provides you with resources and knowledge to move forward as a means of support. To continue to have hard conversations when needed and to balance the things that come with practical tools. Throughout this section, we will discuss a variety of topics, from finding a good healer to understanding myths associated with suicidality.

Here are some tips for finding a good therapist and other healing modalities. You work with these topics together—both the person in crisis and the support person.

Don't settle.

Find what works for you.

Explore options, try something, and if it doesn't resonate, try something else.

Be engaged in the work of recovery.

If you get referrals, get them from someone you feel would want the same type of modality the person in crisis might want. Sometimes people refer friends or colleagues without much thought as to whether the person asking for the referral would find success. If possible, ask someone who gets the needs and has engaged in healing practices for a referral.

Try more than one way of healing. Maybe a yoga class and traditional therapy, or acupuncture and somatic practices, might work. There are many paths to healing, so be open to finding what works.

Together make a list of what you want to get out of therapy and tell your therapist or healer. Refer to your list when feeling stuck, when you're going nowhere, or when you are off-track.

If you are helping someone find treatment, ask them what they need, what they want, and what they want to explore. You are not the leader; you are the support.

I have a friend who was considering suicide a while ago; once they realized they needed help, they started going to groups and group therapy. They soon found that they didn't resonate with the messaging of the group and the reasons why people had started attending the groups. This means that the reasons why they were there were very different from those of the other members. It wasn't a fit. Then they decided to go to a group that was, demographically, not a close match for them, but the group was on their wavelength. In this unlikely group, they found a place where they could talk openly about their struggles with people who felt similar. This was how they got out of their hard place, through connections with folks that others might have considered "not the right fit."

For the person in crisis. Support groups can be a safe healing space that also allows you and the person you are helping to build community. They can be places to lean on your community for support, especially if you feel the other communities you are associated with might need help understanding where you are coming from. Finding the right group takes time. You may go to a few before you find a group that resonates with you. Don't just go one time and judge a group. Give it a few sessions before you decide if it is working or not.

If you can't find a group that works for you, you might look online or create one yourself. A group doesn't have to be a lot of people;

you can start an intimate group of one or two other folks if that seems safer. This information can also be applied to the person you are helping, understanding that they may need a different group than you might choose.

Lean on your communities if you can. When you need to rest, do so. Don't spend so much time fretting about everyone else. This is about you first this time. Don't be a jerk to everyone, but prioritize yourself for once. Allow others to help you, check in on you, and give you support. This is hard if you are someone who always takes care of their problems. Try to remember how good it feels to help someone, and allow others to feel that sense when helping you. Allow yourself to be carried when you need it. I am not talking about engaging in gossip. If you are helping someone in need, this is not an action you use to spill the beans about the person, or to judge them, or to disregard their privacy. You can lean on the community without gossip. You can simply say, I need help right now, and the exchange rate is not a juicy tidbit of scandal; it is just an act of supporting me.

Lean on faith and spiritual practices if that is your jam. Even learning a few mindfulness practices will really help as you move through this process. Remember, these are your practices; if you are supporting someone, you need to find out what they do in terms of spirituality and help them find nurturing there. Don't force your ideas on the person in crisis; you will only drive them away. As you support someone, you will need help. If you have a strong faith in something, use it as a resting place.

Get ready for emotions. There will be a lot of them. Some will hit you square in the face, and it will sting. Some days, you will wonder if it has broken you or if you have reached the end (whatever that is), but know it is coming, and be prepared, realizing much of the emotion is a release. It might be a river of tears that becomes an ocean. It might be anger so hot and overwhelming it has the power to disintegrate everything in its path. It might show up as a vast desert of sadness.

For the support person. Remember, there is no space for toxic positivity. There is no need to say things like, "Get over it," "You'll find another person to love someday," or anything like that. Instead, find meaningful things to say, like, "I am sorry this hurts so bad," "I don't understand how you feel, but I am here for you," and "What do you need from me? What can I do for you right now?"

Realize that the stereotypes and historical perspectives on suicidal ideation and treatments are not truths. A huge part of what you think you know about suicide is not true and can actually be harmful.

The Mayo Clinic identifies eight myths around suicide.

1. **Talking about suicide increases the chances that a person will attempt suicide.** In fact, the opposite may be more accurate. Allowing open dialogue destigmatizes suicidal ideation and creates a space for people to discuss their feelings and ways to address these thoughts. It creates an open dialogue for treatment and acceptance.

2. **People who talk about suicide are just trying to get attention; it isn't real.** It takes a lot for someone to come out and say something about ending their life. Even if they are saying it in a joking way, it should always be taken seriously. Some people who are struggling will joke about it to test the waters, to see if people will be judgmental about the topic.

3. **Suicide cannot be prevented.** Suicide is preventable, but it is also unpredictable. The person suffering may be experiencing a host of different mental and physical concerns.

4. **People who take their own lives are selfish, or weak, or cowards.** This one I hate the most. Dying by suicide is not a choice someone is making using a fully functional mind. They often feel that this is the only way. Some people who have attempted suicide often report they felt that they were such a significant burden on others that they thought this would help people. The thought was totally unselfish. Death by suicide isn't a causal choice to spite someone or because they can't do something or overcome something. The thoughts are not often rooted in rational thinking. Often, people have other mental health concerns such as depression, delusion, or substance abuse issues.

5. **Young people, teenagers, and college kids are most at risk.** Nope, all age groups are at risk. The stats show that older folks also have high percentages. People in specific demographics have a higher rate than teens and young adults in other demographics.

6. **Limits and barriers to firearms, bridges, and other lethal weapons don't work.** Studies have shown that reduced access to lethal weapons, or to bridges without nets, saves lives. Creating barriers to access allows a space for someone to pause before attempting suicide.

7. **There are no warning signs for suicide.** There are always warning signs. Please see the Warning Signs section for more information.

8. **Therapy, meditation, and other forms of help don't work.** Again untrue. This can be especially true when someone is suffering from depression, bipolar disorder, mental illness, extreme grief and overwhelm, or abuse. Finding a modality that works can take time, as I mentioned above, but it will help.

Suicide did not become a central issue in the US until the mid-1990s. Grassroots organizations made up of those who had survived suicide, using the UN guidelines for national strategy, pushed for the US to take up such work. In 1999, a conference was held, and key points were established.

1. Suicide prevention must recognize and affirm the value, dignity, and importance of each person.

2. Suicide is not solely the result of illness or inner conditions. The feelings of hopelessness that contribute to suicide can stem from societal conditions and attitudes. Therefore, everyone concerned with suicide prevention shares a responsibility to help change attitudes and eliminate the conditions of oppression, racism, homophobia, discrimination, and prejudice.

3. Some groups are disproportionately affected by these societal conditions, and some are at greater risk for suicide.

4. Individuals, communities, organizations, and leaders at all levels should collaborate to promote suicide prevention.

5. The success of this strategy ultimately rests with individuals and communities across the US.

In the early 2000s, significant legislation was enacted, calling for more studies. Federal grants were made available for suicide prevention work, and in 2001, national hotlines were created, as well as a national resource center.

Work continues, and statistics are gathered. More work needs to continue toward a less stigmatized and taboo outlook on suicide. Being able to openly discuss mental illness, social problems, abuse, and other taboo subjects that drastically impact our lives is vital work. It impacts our ability to live full and fulfilling lives. If we can't discuss these things, we leave so many people at risk for not only death, but other abusive outcomes.

Substance abuse can play a role in suicide attempts and completion by increasing the likelihood of suicide, but it is, in itself, not a direct cause. It dulls the ability to think clearly and creates a host of physical issues that impede clear thinking. Many people partake of substances before their attempt or completion of suicide, often to dull thinking and thus allowing them to move forward with the process.

Many people self-medicate with substances instead of addressing the real undercurrent of the reasons for medication. For example, people with depression, low self-esteem, and grief may turn to drugs or alcohol to deaden those feelings when they become unbearable.

Drugs like opiates can provide a calming effect that is desirable when looking for an escape.

People with chronic pain will use substances to reduce the effect and provide temporary relief.

According to the *American Journal of Psychiatry*, "Collectively, substance use disorders confer a risk of suicide that is ten to fourteen times greater than that of the general population; deaths related to substance use are highest among persons with alcohol use disorders followed by persons who abuse opiates."

The media's portrayal of suicide also creates confusion and misunderstanding. It is hard to convey the complexities of suicide in a two-hour movie or a mini-series or to sum up all the facets in a blog post. This book won't even do it justice. If you watch media about suicide, they are often filled with myths and stereotypes.

Only the brooding teen who was laughed at in the hallway
attempts suicide. Only homeless and down-and-out people
self-medicate and attempt suicide. Only unhappy people think of
suicide. But the truth is that suicide is a possibility for all bodies.
No one is immune. Some may be more prone to suicidal thoughts
due to various things we will discuss later, but no one is immune.
You can't have enough money, fame, friends, family, happiness,
things, or whatever to grant you immunity. If you think someone
is suffering, there is a chance you are right, so reach out to them.
They may not tell you right away, but you have positioned yourself
as a safe place to go when they are ready to talk. Continue to
check in on them. Consider yourself an ally. You may say or do the
wrong thing once in a while, but that is part of the process. It is
okay to mess up; just correct your course when needed.

How do you check in with folks during and after an episode? "An
episode" makes it sound like an isolated situation, but that is not
always the case. Often, what brings us to suicidal thoughts is a
web of many things. We may feel good one day and go back to
those same old feelings the next. Having someone check in with
us can be very irritating and can provoke anger. The check-in
might feel more like toxic positivity than like help. I suggest you
discuss checking in with each other. Come up with a system for
checking in; ask what the person would like you to say or how they
would like to be approached. If they tell you "Nothing," that is not
a good answer; they need to help you know how to engage in a
way that feels safe and understanding. Sometimes, a code phrase
is a good idea to warn you when you are in social situations. I used
a strategy like this when my kids were teenagers and they went to
parties. If they felt unsafe, they would say their mom was texting
them, and they had to check in to avoid problems, then they would
say to me, "Yes, I fed the dog." This phrase meant "Come pick me
up," which I would. It allowed them to save face at a party, but
also to exit and be safe. The blame for having to leave fell on me,

not them. In creating this system, we used cues that only a few people knew. In doing so, we avoided unwanted conversations with eavesdroppers. It was a reminder for me to practice non-judgment. In creating this space, it opened up a dialogue that might have never happened otherwise. Because of the neutral space created, free and open discussion could take place. They also knew they had a safety net if things went sideways.

The most important thing to remember is that this is a partnership of support, not a hierarchy. You are collaborating on positive outcomes. You are not dictating the rules.

Some folks ask, is it possible to "heal" from suicidal thoughts? I wouldn't be truthful if I didn't tell you that sometimes I find those old thoughts rambling around in my head: "It's too hard," "Life is too hard," "People don't like me," "I am alone," but I recognize these old friends as a pattern of thinking that was once my only company during hard times. Sometimes, when I am driving by a cliff, I feel the familiar notion of, "What if I just drove off it? Can I ensure death?" But these thoughts have little or no weight to them anymore. They are old patterns resurfacing, and I remind myself that I have new tools. As I mentioned in the first section, Zen philosophy turned the tide for me. Living into the notion that I could not be happy with something but still be okay with where I am was a game changer for me. To live into that belief with my whole body and not just as a rational thought I had memorized.

That said, I do believe it is possible to heal from suicidal thoughts. It involves realizing and understanding that the body holds onto patterns and the familiar, whether it is serving you or not. The sympathetic nervous system is always on the lookout for potential hurt and pain and sometimes responds in a knee-jerk fashion. It doesn't scroll through your Rolodex of things you have learned and thoughtfully pick out the best way to handle a thought; it looks to the well-worn paths as a place to run.

It is important to unbecome what you became by recognizing what doesn't serve. You may never be able to completely let go of things because your body is retaining a lot of your history. The key is to recognize the old patterns when they arise and realize that they have now become external feelings that visit you from time to time to discuss the past. They do not live with you anymore, in your house, in your body; they have simply come to visit. Let them know they are part of who you were; for that, you have respect, but they are no longer part of the governing body. They are villagers who live outside of town. They come in every once in a while to grab a bite to eat and then go back to the country. These old feelings do not have to become outcasts or be locked away in cages for all eternity. For me, that manifested into shame. Instead, I understand that these feelings, while they hold no truth as I once thought, can be present in the capacity of how they shaped me into who I am. I am grateful in a way. I received gifts, like writing this book, which would not have been possible had I not experienced it myself. I can embrace these old thoughts and beliefs as a part of my past, but they don't cross the threshold into the present. They no longer have validity with me, but I do have reverence for the very hard, long, treacherous journey that I took with them.

For me, healing was about accepting myself, my thoughts, and my emotions, letting go of the grief and unhappiness, and not allowing the parts that used to dictate my reality to have that kind of power anymore. But I am also grateful for this human journey and that I didn't just go to Disneyland while I was here on Earth; I also went on an expedition into the uncharted and lived to talk about it.

The person you are supporting can heal from this situation, but remember, you are a collaborator. People can't get beyond a self-definition if others are constantly trying to drag them back to something they once were. People need the space and luxury to redefine things, and you will need to honor that. If someone you love comes out to you, and you are struggling with it, understand this: Their pain is related to people they love not accepting them. Accept even what you don't understand. If you want healing to take place, people need to come as they are. People need to be their authentic selves. If you cannot be your genuine self to the people you love, then it is, in a sense, denying who you are. This will foster self-hatred, low self-esteem, imposter syndrome, identity loss, and so many other things. If someone tells you something about themselves and confides in you an inner belief or definition, honor it. If someone decides to take a path you wouldn't take, honor it. Unless what they are doing is very dangerous and irrational, honor their confidences. Be loyal and truthful with your struggles to understand and seek knowledge from other people in confidential ways. If your child comes out as queer and you can't understand, it is your job to understand. Find someone who can help you with this. As I said in the beginning, you must come to these pages with complete openness. You cannot help someone if you are judgmental or controlling. I have never seen kicking a child out of the house as having a positive impact on someone; in fact, often, it opens them up to more dangers and distress. I have seen kids who have gotten kicked out and find a positive place to live, but rejection is so incredibly damaging; even if they find safety in living, their minds can become killers if they feel unwanted. I cannot stress enough that if you make someone feel small, unwanted, powerless, lesser than, or discounted, you are going to create an internal environment within that person that is destructive. Are you going to cause more damage than is already there, and why? To be right? This isn't a third-grade spelling bee; this is a person's life.

Being right isn't even part of the equation. Who gives a shit about being right? It is about the person you picked up this book to help. It is about helping someone survive.

Speaking of stereotypes related to suicide, here are some facts from the CDC that illustrate how different groups may be more at risk. You will find some of this surprising.

In 2021, 12.3 million adults thought about suicide (and that was just from those who reported; so many do not). Of that, 2.5 million made a plan, and 1.7 million adults attempted suicide.

Men are more likely to attempt suicide than women are. Men make up 50 percent of the population but 80 percent of suicides. Age also plays a role; the highest suicide rates are with people seventy-five years old and older. People twenty-five to thirty-five years old also are more likely than someone younger.

Firearms are used in more than 50 percent of suicides, thus being the agent of choice. This could be due to the accessibility to a firearm vs other methods.

According to the CDC website, particular populations, or groups of folks, experience more negative conditions or factors related to suicide due to, in part, harmful social conditions, being veterans, people who live in rural areas, sexual and gender minorities, middle-aged adults, BIPOC folx, and tribal populations. The excess burden of suicide in some populations is a form of what are called health disparities.

Negative factors where people live, play, work, and learn can also play a role in suicide and suicidal thoughts. These factors, sometimes referred to as social determinants of health, encapsulate a wide array of issues, for example, racism and discrimination, economic hardship, poverty, limited affordable housing, lack of educational opportunities, barriers to physical and mental healthcare access, high unemployment rates, immigration status, and other hardships. Other factors can include relationship issues or feeling a lack of connectedness to others, easy access to lethal means, violence, child abuse and neglect, childhood traumas, bullying, and serious health conditions.

Add on an additional factor if you are not part of the normative culture. According to the Trevor Project, LGBTQ+ youth are at a higher risk of suicide solely because they are mistreated and stigmatized. This population would not be as vulnerable if they were free of society's mistreatment and abuse. According to the Trevor Project, LGBTQ+ young people are more than four times as likely to attempt suicide as their peers (Johns et al., 2019; Johns et al., 2020). The Trevor Project estimates that more than 1.8 million LGBTQ+ young people (ages thirteen to twenty-four) seriously consider suicide each year in the US, and at least one attempts suicide every forty-five seconds.

The Trevor Project's 2023 US National Survey on the Mental Health of LGBTQ Young People found that 41 percent of LGBTQ+ young people seriously considered attempting suicide in the past year, including roughly half of transgender and nonbinary youth.

The concept of otherness needs to be mentioned here. When people read the statistics, they often subconsciously read the demographics through the lens of otherness. "Otherness" or "othering" refers to one group defining individuals or groups as not part of their group. It might be that the group or individuals have different customs, beliefs, attributes, or even live in different places. This contributes to the us-vs-them mentality.

Othering can also result in developing negative perspectives and beliefs about a different group of people simply because they are not part of a certain subgroup. Typically, you hear things like, "They are not like us" or "They are different from me." People might consider others less worthy or less human or not as capable or smart. It is part of the process that dehumanizes larger groups of folks in the form of prejudice, racism, sexism, ageism, and negative views toward queer communities. As a result, these marginalized groups are less likely to have access to certain spaces, are more likely to be denied rights, are more susceptible to exploitation, are excluded from opportunities, and so on. The act of othering can be isolating for people when they feel that a judgment is being made simply because they are not exactly like the group that is judging.

What are some of the signs? They may be very subtle. People may have internal biases that they are blind to. They may deny that they are othering because they can't look at their own biases and reflect on their own thinking.

Some examples might be that members of a group define themselves with positive qualities, but those outside of the group are characterized by negative attributes. Think of mean girls or the popular kids from movies. Sometimes people believe groups or individuals are out to get them, to be feared, distrusted, watched, or are dangerous, for no other reason than because they are different. I always think of the example Obama gave from when he was young; he was aware that white people would often cross the street if he were walking toward them, to avoid him out of fear. Fear that was based on internal biases about people who weren't white like them. Outright refusal to interact or accept certain folks into a group simply because you have decided that those people do not belong. Not seeing people as individuals, but rather as the group you associate them with. These are just a few of the signs of othering. When you create an "us and them" system, you deny folks dignity, inclusion, and equality. This can severely limit access to things someone needs.

Internal biases categorize people as "other" based on age, disabilities, gender identity, sex, ethnicity, nationality, race, language, political or religious affiliations, skin color and other physical features, socioeconomic status, language, and even where a person lives. When reading statistics around suicide, or basically anything, it is important to keep in mind that the information is not to be used to emphasize how we differ from each other. For example, some folks tend to look at statistics based on these categories and think, "I am not in that age group, so I don't care about them," or discount a group of people who are suffering simply because they fall into a category that person has othered. But everybody represented in these statistics is important. They matter to me, to you, to society, communities, nations, groups, families, loved ones, friends, acquaintances, and so on. Everyone has value.

How we treat others has a huge impact on suicide rates. When this impact is negative, it is a definite failing of a society that prides itself on knowledge and acceptance.

These facts alone don't save someone, but they are a wake-up call to those who know someone suffering and for those of us trying to help someone who is suffering. They are a sober reminder that our treatment of others plays a profound role in their lives and ripples through communities well beyond the isolated incidents of mistreatment that may happen behind closed doors, in locker rooms, bars, and our own homes.

Another thing I am always mindful of is that, although so many people consider suicide every year, with numbers continuing to rise, far fewer actually attempt it. I can't help but believe that people supporting others have brought down that statistic. Often, suicide is preventable. The loss of a loved one is, however, forever. If you are on the fence about helping someone or reaching out, I urge you to put your reservations aside and do something. Be there, be kind, be helpful, and be a collaborator for health. It will be hard. I am not denying it. But if you can help someone, it is possible.

As the statistics above clearly show, suicide prevention is an intersectional, political act as much as it is a mental health "issue." Standing up for equality, equity, and diversity can help reduce suicide rates. Standing up for marginalized and stigmatized folx can be a matter of life and death. Offering ways to change how they deal with trauma and grief can be a lifeline to someone. Changing power dynamics is pivotal to positive change regarding a healthier world for all bodies. We are killing people with our ignorance. Literally, if we don't start understanding and taking critical race theory seriously, we risk more unnecessary deaths.

4.

FOR SURVIVORS OF LOSS RELATED TO SUICIDE

"There are no goodbyes for us. Wherever you are,
you will always be in my heart."

—Mahatma Gandhi

Everything and anything I could say here is trite and hollow. I offer you my heart in reverence for your indescribable pain.

If you are reading this section because you have experienced a loss, I am deeply, deeply sorry. I will never know exactly how you feel because your feelings are unique to you, but I can be here for you on these pages. I understand your grief; I acknowledge it, the great depths of it that can never be fully repaired. I witness your anguish in all of its sorrow and anger, despair, righteousness, and humility. I see you, and I hear you. I know it is far from enough. I urge you to find a support system. Know that whatever comes, it comes. There is no time limit for this grief; there is no going back to normal; things are different now. When you are ready, come back to us as you are. There is acceptance here. If people try to tell you to get over it, tell them to fuck off if you want. I know you will get up when you are ready. Some days will forever be hard, but one day, you will have a day that is okay. And when that happens, you will know that you are starting to heal, but make no mistake, this will leave a vast and ever-noticeable scar on the life you had before, and on everything that ever was.

I am so sorry for your loss. Such trivial words for what happened, I know. I am sorry that words don't exist for this moment. The words are held inside the emotions that spill forth, so let them all come and be here when you can.

For many people, there is an element of shame associated with suicide, despite your societal beliefs. There is no need for shame. This isn't shameful. This is life playing out in an excruciating way.

I offer a few words on working with guilt. It is almost impossible not to feel guilt after someone close to you dies. All the things you should have done, could have done better, flood into your view. You may feel incredible anger toward the one who completed suicide, which will most often morph into grief. Give yourself permission to be angry. It is where you are right now, and often, people feel safer with anger than they do with experiencing grief. It is pretty typical to feel angry at someone who completes suicide, and often, people feel resentful that now they are left to pick up the pieces and deal with what others may think while the person who is dead got off "scot-free." This is common, but it should not be where you stop in the process.

Allow yourself to move through this thing as you are able. Try to understand it from a point of view outside of yourself and your needs. Something dramatic and horrifying happened. It is hard to know what to feel. You will have to deal with the aftermath. You will have to tell people. Some people will judge. Others won't. There is no getting around it. Forget about the "should've's," which means many people feel guilty about what they feel they should have done. "I should have said I love you more," or the biggest one, "I should have picked up the phone," or folks feel that they made the wrong decision: "If only I had checked on them," "If only I had gotten them into seventy-two-hour watch." This is a hindsight game. What you know now is influencing how you feel about a decision you made. Would you have made the same decision knowing what you knew then, without hindsight? It probably seemed right at the time, but now that you have hindsight, you second-guess yourself. If you feel you truly did make a mistake, find a way to work through this. Find help. This is too big to handle alone. It would be best if you had support. Whether it be therapy or something else, find a support system and be honest with yourself; be willing to do this work to heal. Another familiar feeling is one of self-loathing. "I let someone die. I am a horrible person." Again, this stems from the fact that all your processing of the situation is in hindsight. You were doing what you knew to do at the time. Again, all of these are things that, in order to find a healthy life again, you will need to address honestly and with openness. However you choose to address it, find what is right for you. An online grief group might be beneficial to some, while others work on deeper issues through hypnotherapy or other modalities. Whatever works is fine.

One last thing about guilt in relation to pride or perfectionism. Many people, especially parents, find themselves grappling with emotions around needing children to be perfect and being able to use their children for bragging rights around the dinner party table. They may use pride as a conditional response depending on the child's performance on something. Here is one thing I know about this. Your child is always worthy. Perfect doesn't exist. If you live in a culture of competing with your children, I suggest you take a second look at that. It is a setup to make a child feel inferior to others. Let it go. Be proud of them for all the big and little accomplishments they have, even if they don't meet your vision. They are carving their own way, and that takes bravery. Let go of what the other parents will think. Honor your child by remembering their greatness. Let go of the guilt you may have if you felt you held them to high standards. Let it all go; it won't help you here. Be proud of them for all they did. Talk about them in a way that shows your love and admiration.

Many feelings will come through this process. They may be unexpected or come at unpredictable times. Address them as they come with honesty and openness. Grieve until you are done.

Life's different now, and that is okay. When you are ready, come back to us. Don't let the darkness take you too. Fight like hell to stay out of the place your loved one found themselves in. They wouldn't want that for you. I know it is hard. I know it is on the verge of impossible. I know. But don't let go. Come back to us.

How to talk about suicide: tell the truth, say the hard thing. Talking about it will save lives. I know this. The more we talk about suicide mindfully and compassionately, the better we do. By this, I mean don't talk about it as though the deceased was an asshole, or selfish, or any of the other stereotypes and myths. Talk about it in a factual way with truth. If you are suffering, tell people. Talk about your anger, guilt, or shame, and work through your tough emotions. Talk about loss. I talk about loss a lot. I was once told I go to the hard places people don't want to be, and to that, I say, I am trying to save lives here. We all need to develop the skills to sit in the hard place. Life is not always a picnic. Learning the skills to help each other in times of need is essential to the community and the health and well-being of others. The situation that brought someone to complete suicide is so unimaginable and devastating that we struggle with the language for it. How do you find adjectives for the pain the person felt? How do you do the suffering justice? Just start talking. You may never get all the words right, which is okay. We are all learning how to talk about suicide. It is hard but necessary.

Remember that shame thrives on secrecy. Learn how to bring hard things into the light at a rate and pace that is tolerable and supportive, not in a way that enhances shame and keeps people paralyzed in fear. Be supportive and gentle in your speech when it is called for, and use your battle cry when it is needed. Learn how to modulate your communication to be heard, but don't stop talking about it.

Some people use forms of talk therapy to move through this. It helps. Bringing it all out into the light makes it more understandable. You will never truly understand. Only they know how it felt. But you can find a way to make sense of it for yourself.

Know that it is not your fault. There is no fault. That isn't part of this situation. There are only factors that led to this outcome, and even then, the factors are not at fault. As I said, this is a very complex issue, and there are so many factors involved that you will never know them all. This is a horrible and tragic thing that happened. No one and nothing are at fault, not even the person who died. The only fault or outcome is that someone died. Someone died. It is hard because, as humans, we want someone to be at fault for something to direct our anger to deflect the pain. We want someone to pay for this. We want retribution. That isn't helpful here. Someone died; if we blame anything, we need to look to the change we need to make in our society. Change that might have made things more supportive if it could have been made. Again, hindsight is in play here. We only know what we know, but as Maya Angelou, poet and activist, said, "Do the best you can until you know better. Then, when you know better, do better." Once we know this story, we need to tell it in honor of those who suffer; we tell our tales in hope of saving others.

5.

GRIEF

"Grief is a part of Love."

—Megan Devine, *It's OK that You're Not OK*

Grief Is Necessary

*"If we do not grieve what we miss,
we are not praising what we love."*

—Martin Prechtel, *The Smell of Rain on Dust*

Martín Prechtel goes on to say that, after performing a grieving ritual, you leave it. You don't always live in it, but you take the time you need to grieve, and then you begin forward movement.

Come to this section with an openness, as I mentioned at the beginning of the book. Let go of the notion that healing is impossible. Let go of the feeling that you are powerless in this process. Moving forward is possible. You won't be the same, I'll give you that, but you can heal. Healing will not dishonor the person you lost; it will become a way to honor and remember them within a space that doesn't translate into immense pain. Imagine the person you lost. What would they want for you? They would want you to heal. To remember, to laugh, to move forward, to be thoughtful and caring, to enhance the best parts of who you are, and they would want you to heal. They would not want you to suffer. Be open to change. To not identify as the person who lost a loved one, but as someone lucky enough to know a beautiful person. Grief is not part of identity, yet people do internalize it as a character trait. Once this happens, it can be hard to move on, because you have let grief become a personal definition. It's hard to move on from personal definition because we feel the pressure of what other people would think if we weren't this person anymore. What would we think? Would we feel guilty? If so, why? Be open to the process, and be willing to pick up the gifts this process presents. Be willing to do the work.

Bearing Witness to Grief

This means allowing grief to be here and allowing yourself to feel and work with your grief. It does not mean becoming so consumed you can't crawl out of it. Although, at times, it will consume you, it is okay; it is part of the process. To move through hard things, we need to be willing to be with them. Often, spiritual beliefs help here. Try not to use the beliefs as excuses or blame but to use them as a comfort. Use books, stories, ideas, dogma, and concepts as comfort. To soothe your soul and weary body. In Megan Devine's book *It's OK That You're Not OK*, she explains grief as part of love. Love is not just a symptom of losing someone, but is also love for life, for yourself, and for those around you. She goes on to say that what you are experiencing is love, and love can be hard sometimes.

As I mentioned earlier in the book, if you do not allow yourself to move into and through grief, your feelings will take on other forms that are just as painful.

Grief has a tendency to create a pile-on effect, meaning that there is grief from a particular event, and then there are all the connections to that grief that you are still resolving. Maybe the death of a loved one brings up other deaths you have grieved, other losses you have had; on top of that, you may pile on other things in your life that are not resolved, like relationship issues, things you have experienced that didn't go your way, trauma events, the unjust judgment you feel you have received, everything you ever said that you regret, and so on. Abandonment in childhood or earlier in life is often something that gets projected into grief. Are you projecting anything onto your grief? Are you adding older issues to this current grief? You may have to go back to these issues and work with them before you can genuinely grieve your current loss.

Find tenderness for yourself in your grief. Accept it when it comes. Allow yourself to grieve in your own way, but at the same time, try not to let it become overwhelming. A support system is important. Find someone who will allow you to work through grief. Someone who you can be honest with. Have safety mechanisms for yourself. Even simple things like counting to ten, or breathing, or whatever you find soothing can help you manage your grief.

It might help to create a list of things that help you move through grief. Maybe you have a breathing exercise, or you need to learn to pause sometimes. Maybe a warm bath or a funny movie helps. What helps you move from being overwhelmed into having compassion for yourself? What helps you? List those things and refer to the list when needed. Sometimes, in a state of overwhelm, we can't think clearly, and we turn to vices rather than providing nourishment to ourselves. Sometimes, what we think is helping is actually hurting; maybe a walk is better than a glass of wine, or maybe not. Have a list at the ready when overwhelm sets in. This list is flexible; you will add and subtract things as you move within grief. Being flexible is a kindness to yourself. This is a time to practice loving kindness to yourself, because grief often comes with guilt, shame, triggers, overwhelm, depression, withdrawal, second-guessing, and many other feelings that make it hard to be tender with yourself.

Grief Is Natural

There is nothing wrong with you. Grief is a natural response to many things. Grief is how you feel after a loss. It can be a loss of life, but it can also be a loss of a job. Some people experience multiple losses at one time; they may lose a loved one and then lose a job or relationship. Grief is your response to a loss. It is natural, even though it is excruciating at times. Grief will last as long as it lasts. Most likely, you will carry the loss with you throughout your life, but the relationship to the grief will change. When I lost my mother, I was devastated. So many things brought me to regret. So many things to grieve. She left a hole in the lives of all who knew her. It was such an incredible sadness that lasted years. I am still sad sometimes, but my relationship with the grief has become seeing her in things, such as seeing her when I make bread and remembering her cooking and her techniques. I remember her advice, which has taken on new meaning as I get older. I lean on remembering her courage in all things in life. Just writing this down makes me emotional. My point is that my grief has grown into an appreciation for many things and still sadness. I was so overcome with a new wave of grief when my daughters graduated. A moment that my mom wouldn't be able to celebrate with us. It's complicated, but it is part of life. Grief is immense; it may suck you up for a long time. It's okay, take your time. We all experience it differently, and its nuances are unique to each of us, yet similar.

Grief Is Not Meant to Be Borne Alone— It's Too Big

Frequently, I have been told—most recently as of last week— that I occupy uncomfortable places, such as grief, and people don't want to hear about that. It is too hard. It is somehow not acceptable to grieve.

Yet, we all must do the work to allow grief to be expressed. The truth is, we will all experience loss; we will all experience the crippling hold grief has on our bodies and souls. As a community, we need to open a space or spaces for grief to be heard and experienced in all its raw and uncomfortable facets. We need to develop communication that isn't playacting or "tough love"-inspired. We need to celebrate this devotion to a love lost. In essence, we need to be more understanding and compassionate around all expressions of love, including grief. Especially grief. All the hard feelings around love and the complicated concepts that intertwine so intimately with love. Love isn't all hearts and flowers; it is also a tar that permeates with the staying power of a ground-in stain. It doesn't leave you. It comes up now and again, even as you let go of your devotion to daily memories of who you have lost. Even as you let go of constantly trying to keep the person "alive" at the forefront of your mind. Even as the residue of the person collects in the corners, it is still there. As fresh as it was on day one. It is still there. Right now, in your grief, you are where you should be.

The truth is things won't "work out." I don't believe they will; they "get better." It just changes. It becomes part of your lived experience that you carry with you. You can't go back to who you were before the grief; that is simply not the point of it all. You are different now. There is something that resides within that wasn't there before. It will always be painful. To this day, I can't even think about my mother without the feeling of words being caught in my throat and a tear threatening to work its way into a storm. Sometimes I cry about it, even though it has been years now. The hurt is still there. The loss doesn't leave you.

I want you to know that people will not understand. They will want you to move on and go back to "being normal," yet they will whisper about the tragic event to each other. You may feel like you are living in two worlds, expected to be two different people. Turn on the grief when appropriate, like a rally where your experience will have influence, but then turn it off if you are meeting friends for coffee. You turn it on at the therapist's office but turn it off when you go to work. God forbid you haven't turned it off at a social event, but be sure to be the grieving family member or best friend at the funeral.

Often, I hear that people felt bad that they couldn't cry at a funeral or that they were shocked at the lack of emotion when a close family member died. But then, six months later, the grief washed over them like a tsunami, taking all their mental possessions with them and destroying everything in its wake.

About seven years ago, I was going to therapy every week. My routine would be to get in the car at work, drive for an hour on my usual commute home, crying hysterically, all the way to my therapist's office. Then I would spend an hour talking about hard things to a compassionate human, then cry hysterically all the way to my front door (about a fifteen-minute drive). I would collect myself in the driveway and walk into my house. Because even in my sanctuary, my home, I was not free to be who I was at that moment. I was not free to grieve, to be sad, to be devastated, to have unresolved emotions, to feel the shame I felt for not being enough, to come as I was, completely and totally immersed in the dark waters of grief without the ability to swim.

I have often been scolded for being "too sad" or "too mopey," so I learned to put on a face. We take on a mask, but it doesn't heal our soul; it just covers up what we are in the moment because our individualistic society has no framework, words, understanding, or tolerance for anything other than superficial happiness. I often felt like the mayor in *Nightmare Before Christmas*, living in my grief but then switching my face to a smile when someone opened the door.

Be open to the grief of others. Be open to your grief. Find a place where you can come as you are. Bring a lot of tissues and share them generously. Many other people feel like you do. Many brave and beautiful folks are suffering a loss. You are not alone.

Suicide's collective grief extends way beyond the individual life lost. It becomes a collective story about loss and suicide. The statistic is added to national and international statistics. The story becomes a gateway for other stories. I cannot tell you how often, when I tell someone I work with suicide awareness and mental health help, people open up with their own stories of suicide. I have even had bosses tell me incredibly sad stories of suicide in their families. When I am wearing a suicide awareness hoodie, people will come up and tell me their stories. I have heard intimate stories of suicidal thoughts and attempts; others have told me of a recent suicide they heard of in a friend group or family. I venture to think almost everyone you meet has a suicide story of some kind. It weighs heavily on the heart. We are in collective grieving for our loved ones, for ourselves, and alongside those we have never met.

Your grief becomes a community's grief. Many people are profoundly touched by a suicide in their community. Wherever that person exists in the community, the people sharing that space are affected. As we have all seen, when a high schooler dies, the whole school mobilizes, with grief counseling rallies, memorials, and so on. It is a way to work through their grief. Some family and close friends get distraught at this public display, feeling that it lessens the gravity. How do these kids truly understand? But they do. They understand. Perhaps not as profoundly as you do, but in their way, they understand and grieve. It is hard to have a stranger come up to you in the grocery store to tell you how sorry they are. It's hard to feel gratitude when anger is welling up inside. I understand your anger. I do. Frankly, I'd be pissed too. One day, you might need their condolences, but today, you don't. It's fine, you are surviving. It's enough.

People want to support you, and they will do it whether you want it or not. I offer one thought: sometimes you don't want it, but it is also a life preserver. Take it and learn to advocate for what you need. Say, "You can help me, but the help I need today is for you to make me a cup of tea and do the laundry. Don't say anything to me unless I ask you a question. Know that I love you, but that is all I can do today."

"Please drive me to my appointment, but don't ask me one question or say anything to me. We will listen to music, and I will pick the playlist." Say what you need, be grateful, and let them know you love them. That's all you are capable of right now.

For siblings, suffering can be excruciating. Often, after the suicide of a sibling, the child who is alive may not get the attention they need, or may be afraid to ask for it, because everyone else is suffering and unable to help them. They may feel isolated and forgotten, even years afterward. They may find themselves having a hard time making connections with others for fear of loss. They may not work through the grief, living with continual triggering and resurgence of undigested emotions and thoughts. They may also suffer suicidal thoughts due to overwhelm and isolation. Parents may never be the same, and the child may suffer because they don't understand. If the family has a way of being that doesn't discuss certain things or lets things be swept under the rug, a child may be left to figure out what is happening on their own. They may have to come to their own conclusions, which they carry with them throughout life. They may feel unloved and unwanted; they may feel a tremendous amount of guilt or shame. If they are children when the incident happens, they will take a childlike perspective of the situation into adulthood, adopting it as a truth when, in reality, it was a child's perspective and not an accurate picture. They may hate their sibling for what they did. They may have trouble with relationships, work, and other things in life.

They may become overprotective parents, pushing children in unhealthy ways. Many things can happen. The big takeaway here is that siblings experience the loss differently. It is a connection to self that is a more powerful bond. Frequently, siblings experience anger stemming from feelings of abandonment or rejection. They suffer guilt and feelings of not being enough or not knowing.

Siblings may stuff their pain down due to the guilt they feel about overburdening grieving caregivers. They may not want to be another burden, so they suffer in silence. Siblings may feel isolated from the community due to stigma associated with suicide. Their peers may be unable to deal with these issues and, therefore, be unkind or distance themselves. This leaves a sibling with no one to talk to and very limited ways of processing the grief and pain.

Fear of losing a loved one can profoundly affect future relationships, parenting, and work relationships. But if a sibling is given what they need to grieve and understand the situation, and they receive the love and attention they need during this time, they can go on to have meaningful and purposeful lives, often advocating for suicide awareness and other causes.

For Those Supporting Someone in Grief

This is not the time for prevention talk. This is not a time to say things like, "You should have done _____ instead, and this wouldn't have happened." Try not to use the word "should" at all with regard to the person grieving. When you phrase advice in terms of "you should have done" this or that, you run the risk of victim-blaming, which is not helpful at all. Do not blame; it is not the time. I honestly don't think there is ever a time for it. Do not victim-blame other people, either. Don't go telling people that the person grieving should do this, or should have done that. Allow the grief to flow. It needs a place to go.

Blame has no business at this table. Blame implies fault, and fault implies judgment and shame. Someone in the depths of grief does not need the extra weight of shame or guilt. They may blame others in the depths of grief; they may rant and be angry and vent and accuse as they work the process, but it does no good to place blame on the griever. You can bet that, deep down, they are questioning this for themselves; there is no need for you to judge. You are there to witness and support. You are not the judge or the jury.

This will be hard because you are unprepared for it. You can learn how to support people through their grief. You don't have to solve their problems; you can simply support them. Refer to the section on talking about trauma for some tips on what to say about grief. Not all grief is from trauma, but it will give you some great tools for speaking to someone experiencing grief. The most important thing to remember is that you are there, supporting. You aren't the leader; the grieving person will dictate the path; you will carry the bags, use the compass, and scout ahead for places to rest. You will pitch tents, make beds, cook food, do laundry, entertain by the fire, and roll out sleeping bags, but you will not lead unless you are asked to do so. If you are asked to do so, you will not lead with fervor, but with compassion and love. You will lead gently, knowing that it is only temporary; your leader will take back the role soon.

Part IV

ASKING FOR HELP AND UNDERSTANDING WHEN SOMEONE ASKS

"The hunger for love is much more difficult to remove than the hunger for bread."

—Mother Teresa

When people tell you something about their past or a current traumatic situation, it isn't because they want you to feel sorry for them. It is because they are looking for compassion and empathy.

It is because human connection, understanding, and acceptance are all vital to healing. Understanding is the gateway to acceptance. We are hardwired to seek acceptance, and acceptance is love. We are all seeking love because it gives us a sense of belonging. It connects us to a group and allows us to see that past mistakes, or trauma, are a natural part of human life.

Perfection is not part of this experience, no matter what society says. It is impossible to be perfect or reach perfection as a human being. But it is the act of acceptance that allows us to be loved regardless of our past experiences, our mistakes, or any other imperfect part of the human experience.

If someone chooses to tell you something traumatic, they have decided that you are a safe place, and you can help them.

Usually, people don't know how to respond when someone opens up about trauma.

They may change the subject; they may make a pouty face and talk in a baby voice and say, "Oh, I am sorry," or something that may come across as insincere.

They may pat your hand, look away, and move on to a more pleasant topic.

Or they may turn the subject around to something about them.

Maybe it will be about a similar experience they had, or maybe it will be about something they want to talk about involving them. For example, "Let's talk about something fun, like my upcoming BBQ, instead."

They may avoid the person who brought up the traumatic conversation.

They may meet you with toxic positivity by saying things like, "Oh, that isn't so bad" or "That was a long time ago. You should get over it."

We are all guilty of this at one time or another. Do you know why?

Because we are human, and the human experience is full of mistakes and wrong turns.

The human experience is also filled with opportunities to learn, to be sorry, to change, and to gain skills. What we have done in the past when confronted with a friend's trauma does not have to be what we do moving forward.

Two key things are how to receive the conversation and how to create a nonjudgmental space.

In the past, you may not have approached these conversations in a supportive way, and it isn't because you are insensitive or a jerk. Most likely, it is because these conversations are sometimes shocking, devastatingly sad, or overwhelming because talking about trauma has been taboo in the past. Most people lack the skills to talk about it. When the subject comes up, we simply have no language or familiarity to speak about trauma effectively.

Not knowing how to talk about trauma leaves the person dealing with trauma in the space of feeling alone. This leads to feelings of being unloved, being separate, feeling different, feeling shame and unworthiness, and feeling isolated.

1.

TALKING ABOUT TRAUMA IS IMPORTANT

Not talking about trauma can lead to addictive behaviors, inability to deal with conflict, anxiety, depression, PTSD, physical and mental illness, and an innate belief that we have no value.

Here are some things you or a person struggling with trauma can say to open a conversation:

- "There is something I am struggling to move past. I know I need to talk about it to overcome it and move forward, but I am afraid to talk about it because I am afraid I will be judged or that people will think I am overreacting."

- "I need to tell you something about my past so I can start working toward healing. If I tell you, will you listen and not judge me or think I am making too much of it?"

- "I am struggling with something in my past that I can't get over. I need to move on. Can you help me by listening to me in a nonjudgmental space? I don't want to be told that I am overreacting or should get over it. I just need someone to listen and hear me. To see me. To hear me."

Or something like that. Mix and match the things that work best for you. The first time you ask for a nonjudgmental space, you may feel silly or strange, but the more you do it, the easier it becomes. The more you talk about your trauma in a space where you are heard and not judged, the more possibility there is for you to heal.

Having the language to help someone is important. It can be the breakthrough they need to move through the thing that is holding them back. Knowing how to react or be present is helpful for the listener because it gives them the tools they need to be present.

Here are some tips for being the listener in a conversation about trauma:

- Allow the person to speak even if it is upsetting to them. Let them tell you all they need to know without judgment or trying to fix the issue. Just listen.

- Don't insist they need professional help. Not everyone who is a survivor of trauma needs therapy. Do not offer solutions unless they ask. Again, your job is only to listen.

- Refrain from bringing up your own experiences. You may do this if asked about it or at a later time, but not now. This conversation is not about you.

- Don't expect a person to get over it.

- Be nonjudgmental.

- Don't meet them with toxic positivity.

- Don't think you know how they feel; the experience is unique to each individual.

- Be empathetic.

- Don't avoid talking about the event.

- Don't think you know how someone would behave. Each person is different. Some people will laugh or smile when talking about trauma.

- Most people need to talk about trauma in bursts or multiple conversations. Let them know you are always here for them.

- Again, don't judge.

- Don't turn it into a solutions-based conversation—like trying to solve the problem—unless they ask.

- Say things like, you are loved just as you are.

- Say things like, I hear you; I am here for you. You are not alone.

- You are human; being human means things aren't perfect, and that's okay.

- You do not need to do anything else to be valid; you already are.

- Do not touch the person unless you have a relationship where that is a positive experience for them.

- Ask if you can hold their hand, hug them, or put your arm around them. Don't assume this will be helpful.

Things not to say:

- It is time to move on.

- That was a long time ago.

- Stop being so negative.

- Why are you letting this affect you?

- It was not that bad.

- If you continue to dwell on it, then you will never move on.

- Do you think you will ever stop being depressed about this?

- You are a survivor. Quit being a victim.

- It could be worse.

- That was a long time ago. Get over it.

- No one wants to know this about this. (Don't tell anyone this—in fact, they should talk about it to heal.)

- Do not talk about your own issues unless asked about them.

- Do not make conversation about your issues.

- Punitive language or ideas aren't the answer.

- Some people have challenges with the phrase "commit suicide" and, therefore, try to avoid the phrase.

Do say:

- I am here for you.

- I don't know how it feels to go through what you have, but I can be here for you.

- I am sorry that you are going through this. I am here if more comes up.

- Can I help you in any way?

- I love you.

- I am here for you.

- I support you.

- I understand how hard this is.

- You were brave to tell me, and I appreciate what you did.

- I don't know what to say to make this better for you, but I hear you. I see you.

- You matter. You matter to me and to everyone you know.

- You are enough just as you are. Really, I mean that.

- What do you need?

- How can I be here for you?

- That took a lot of courage to open up to me, and I value your strength.

- You are a good person.

- I am touched by your ability to tell me things that might have been hard to say.

- You are not alone.

- Your story matters.

- You matter to me.

These conversations are hard, but they are okay. No matter what happens, it is okay.

Ask them if they need help, and if so, what help? Let them tell you what they need.

These conversations are complicated and complex and can also be triggering. Make sure you take care of yourself. Hearing about a loved one's trauma can be traumatic in itself, and knowing how to take care of yourself is essential.

If the person seems to be suicidal or struggling with suicidal thoughts, you can call the suicide hotline in your area (listed in the comments below). It's 988 in the US. You can get them into a seventy-two-hour watch or call a healer and schedule an appointment. You can go to the appointment with them if needed.

Ask them if they have any contacts they would like to share with you in case of an emergency. This might include emergency numbers (family or friends), work numbers, doctors or therapists, healers, or other health-related folks. Assure them you will not contact anyone unless it is an emergency, but you will keep the numbers handy for now because you have their back. You are here for them.

It is hard to be there for people because society does not promote such work, but it is important for us to break that mold and be there for each other.

When it is hard, tell people.

When you are struggling, tell someone.

We can be in this together. We can help each other.

We can make a difference for ourselves and everyone else.

It is possible to change the culture to something kinder and more caring.

We are human, and humans need other humans.

We are hardwired for this. Modern culture sometimes puts too much emphasis on things that create individuality and aloneness.

The real power lies in human connection.

Our superpower isn't how we can do things alone but how we can unite and heal the wounds that make us human.

Our superpower is exactly what humans are hardwired to desire. Our superpower is love and kindness.

Love means openness; it means humility, vulnerability, collaboration, respect, dignity, forgiveness, and understanding.

Love creates meaning and a will to survive. Love is a purpose and a place to rest. Come to your life and the people you care about with love. This is going to be a journey. It will take a lot out of you. At times, you will literally fight for your life. People may not be that supportive or may be ignorant of what you are going through. People may even be cruel. You will need support. You might feel lost now and again. Circle back to the love. Open your heart to yourself and those helping you.

Human connection is a primal need. Feed yourself, even when you feel all you want to do is lie in bed and melt.

If you are supporting someone, let them lead. Be patient, be understanding. Take care of yourself too. Be kind to yourself, know your limits, know your capacity, and gather resources.

Welcome all the emotions to your table, and know that they will leave once the visit is over. They may stay a while, but they will go.

This will not be easy. This is possible. You can find a path forward.

2.

A WORD ON HOPE

Frankly, I wouldn't say I like to use this word, because it implies a future time frame: you hope you will get better, rather than, I am better every day, I am healing, I am worthy of a beautiful life. I am worthy of laughter and friends and happiness and fulfillment. I am worthy of a body without a state of overwhelm or feelings of inadequacy. I am enough just as I am right now.

To me, these statements are more constructive. And you know what? I wholeheartedly believe them to be true for you.

For those folks who are supporting people in this journey, you too must adopt healing in the present moment. It isn't something you will get to one day; you are there now. Just by reading this book, you are choosing to heal, to support healing, and to move toward a future.

No hope is necessary; courage, curiosity, openness, love, and gentleness are the tools. The rest will become.

Part V

RESOURCE GUIDE

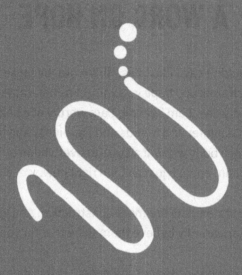

SOME RISK FACTORS

Taken from Very Well Mind, CDC, and National Institute for Mental Health.

- Death or terminal illness of a relative or friend
- Divorce, separation, or the breakup of a relationship
- Loss of health (real or imagined)
- Loss of job, home, money, status, self-esteem, or personal security
- Drug or alcohol misuse
- Depression
- Previous suicide attempts
- Holidays and anniversaries
- The first week after discharge from the hospital
- When treatment with an antidepressant first begins
- Just before and after diagnosis of a major illness (for example, the risk of suicide in cancer patients is highest shortly after diagnosis, rather than after cancer has spread or progressed)
- Just before and during disciplinary proceedings
- Violence victimization and/or perpetration
- Bullying
- Family/loved one's history of suicide
- Loss of relationships
- High-conflict or violent relationships
- Social isolation
- Lack of access to healthcare
- Suicide cluster in the community
- Stress of acculturation
- Community violence
- Historical trauma
- Discrimination
- The stigma associated with help-seeking and mental illness
- Easy access to lethal means of suicide among people at risk
- Unsafe media portrayals of suicide

CIRCUMSTANCES THAT PROTECT AGAINST SUICIDE RISK

These personal factors protect against suicide risk:

- Effective coping and problem-solving skills
- Reasons for living (for example, family, friends, pets, etc.)
- Strong sense of cultural identity

These healthy relationship experiences protect against suicide risk:

- Support from partners, friends, and family
- Feeling connected to others

These supportive community experiences protect against suicide risk:

- Feeling connected to school, community, and other social institutions
- Availability of consistent and high-quality physical and behavioral healthcare

These cultural and environmental factors within the larger society protect against suicide risk:

- Reduced access to lethal means of suicide among people at risk
- Open dialogue and safety

SOME WARNING SIGNS

- Using speaking points or phrases associated with suicide, death, harm, or other related topics. Discussing these topics often makes it seem as though they are always thinking about them.

- Uncharacteristic conversations about dying, death, wanting to die, people who have completed suicide, and suicide in general.

- Talking about feeling guilty or having shame. Hating oneself.

- Talking about being a burden.

- Talking about not having friends or anyone who cares about them.

- Feeling empty, hopeless, trapped, or having no reason to live.

- Extremely sad, more anxious, agitated, or full of rage.

- Having unbearable emotional or physical pain.

- Changing behavior patterns, such as planning or researching ways to die, withdrawing from friends, saying goodbye, giving away important items, or making a will.

- Taking dangerous risks, such as driving extremely fast, or engaging in dangerous acts, like jumping off bridges or standing at the threshold of a tall building.

- Displaying extreme mood swings.

- Eating or sleeping more or less than is normal for them.

- Using drugs or alcohol more often.

- Preoccupation with death.

- Statements like, "You would be better off without me" or "I wish I were dead."

- Talking openly about wanting to kill oneself.

- Development of a suicide plan, acquiring the means to carry it out, "rehearsal" behavior, or setting a time for the attempt.

- Making out a will or giving away favorite possessions.

- Inappropriately saying goodbye.

- Making ambiguous statements like, "You won't have to worry about me anymore," "I wish I could go to sleep and never wake up," or "I just can't take it anymore."

- Suddenly switching from being very depressed to being very happy or calm for no apparent reason.

- Not performing well in school, work, or other activities.

- Becoming socially isolated or falling in with the "wrong crowd."

- Declining interest in sex, friends, or activities previously enjoyed.

- Neglecting personal welfare or letting their appearance go.

- Experiencing a change in eating or sleeping habits.

WHAT TO DO AND WHEN

- Please refer to Part IV.

- Remember to listen; don't judge.

- Ask what they need.

- Validate how they are feeling.

- Offer support.

- Create a safety plan (template in the appendix).

GETTING SOMEONE INTO A SEVENTY-TWO-HOUR WATCH

A seventy-two-hour hold is an involuntary admittance to a seventy-two-hour mental health hold if your doctor feels that you pose a danger to yourself or others or you are unable to provide food and shelter for yourself. This is not something you tap into unless there is a serious threat. It can be helpful if you feel there is a real threat.

You are kept at a facility for seventy-two hours or less if you are no longer a threat to yourself or others.

The program varies depending on where you are.

In the state of California, for example, a healthcare professional must admit you.

Consult with a doctor in your area to find out the facts about the program in your area.

In the appendix, you will find the state of California's seventy-two-hour Mental Health Involuntary Hold information. The full explanation can be found at Nami.org.

QUICK GUIDE—A FEW IDEAS ON WHAT TO SAY AND NOT TO SAY

Taken from Part IV as a quick reference guide.

- Don't expect a person to get over it.

- Be nonjudgmental.

- Don't meet them with Toxic Positivity.

- Don't think you know how they feel; the experience is unique to each individual.

- Be empathetic.

- Don't avoid talking about the event.

- Don't think you know how someone would behave. Each person is different. Some people will laugh or smile when talking about trauma.

- Most people need to talk about trauma in bursts or multiple conversations. Let them know you are always here for them.

- Again, don't judge.

- Don't turn it into a solutions-based conversation—like trying to solve the problem—unless they ask.

- Say things like, you are loved just as you are.

- Say things like, I hear you; I am here for you. You are not alone.

- You are human; being human means things aren't perfect, and that's okay.

- You do not need to do anything else to be valid; you already are.

- Do not touch the person unless you have a relationship where that is a positive experience for them.

- Ask if you can hold their hand, hug them, or put your arm around them. Don't assume this will be helpful.

GUIDE TO SOME OF THE NATIONAL ORGANIZATIONS WORKING ON SUICIDE AWARENESS AND PREVENTION

This guide is incomplete, as many grassroots organizations are doing good work, and many may be local to you.

Mental Illness and Health

- Nami.org (mental health programs)
- www.cdc.gov/suicide/facts/index.html (CDC)
- www.2020mom.org/ (policy, training, resources)
- www.who.int/data/gho/data/themes/mental-health/suicide-rates (World Health Organization)
- www.nimh.nih.gov/health/topics/suicide-prevention (National Institute of Mental Health)

Grief

- Grief.com

Suicide Prevention and Awareness

- Save.org
- 988lifeline.org (national hotline)
- youmatter.988lifeline.org (for teens)

- www.crisistextline.org (texting hotline)

- afsp.org/about-afsp (National Foundation for Suicide Awareness)

- suicidology.org/about-aas-2 (American Association of Suicidology (AAS))

- www.thetrevorproject.org (Trevor Project LGBTQ+)

- twloha.com (high school programs, awareness)

- www.preventsuicidemke.com/about.html (a program of NAMI providing programming and resources for the Milwaukee area)

- www.socialrefugees.org (programming, resources, grassroots)

- www.suicidestop.com/call_a_hotline.html (resources and therapy)

- pausefirst.com/about (resources and training for first responders)

APPENDIX

VIA Institute on Character, examples of virtues
www.viacharacter.org/character-strengths

USA

- 988 Suicide and Crisis Lifeline: 988 or Lifeline Chat
- Crisis Text Line: Text HOME TO 741741

Emergency Numbers Worldwide

Thank you to the International Bipolar Foundation for compiling this list. It can be found online at: ibpf.org/resource/list-of-international-suicide-hotlines

Argentina: +5402234930430

Australia: 131114

Austria: 017133374

Belgium: 106

Botswana: 3911270

Brazil: 212339191

Canada

- 5147234000 (Montreal)

- 18662773553 (outside Montreal)

China: 85223820000

Croatia: 014833888

Denmark: +4570201201

Egypt: 7621602

Finland: 040-5032199

France: 0145394000

Germany: 08001810771

Holland: 09000767

India: 8888817666

Ireland: +4408457909090

Italy: 800860022

Japan: +810352869090

Mexico: 5255102550

New Zealand: 045861048

Norway: +4781533300

Philippines: 028969191

Poland: 5270000

Russia: 0078202577577

Spain: 914590050

South Africa: 0514445691

Sweden: 46317112400

Switzerland: 143

United Kingdom: 08457909090

United States

- Emergency 911

- Suicide Hotline 988

- More Hotlines: blog.
  opencounseling.com/
  hotlines-us
- In-Person Counseling:
  blog.opencounseling.com/
  location_search

Algeria

- Emergency 34342 and 43
- Suicide Hotline 0021
  3983 2000 58

Angola: Emergency 113

Argentina

- Emergency 911
- Suicide Hotline 135

Armenia

- Emergency 911 and 112
- Suicide Hotline (2) 538194

Australia

- Emergency 000
- Suicide Hotline 131114
- More Hotlines: blog.
  opencounseling.com/
  hotlines-au
- In-Person Counseling:
  blog.opencounseling.com/
  location_search

Austria

- Emergency 112
- Telefonseelsorge 24/7 142
- Rat auf Draht 24/7
  147 (Youth)

Bahamas

- Emergency 911
- Suicide Hotline (2) 322-2763

Bahrain

- Emergency 999
- More Hotlines: blog.
  opencounseling.com/
  hotlines-bh
- In-Person Counseling:
  blog.opencounseling.com/
  location_search

Bangladesh

- Emergency 999
- More Hotlines: blog.
  opencounseling.com/
  hotlines-bd
- In-Person Counseling:
  blog.opencounseling.com/
  location_search

Barbados

- Emergency 911
  Suicide Hotline

- Samaritan Barbados
  (246) 4299999

Belgium

- Emergency 112

- Suicide Hotline Stichting
  Zelfmoordlijn 1813

Bolivia

- Emergency 911

- Suicide Hotline 3911270

- More Hotlines: blog.
  opencounseling.com/
  hotlines-bo

- In-Person Counseling:
  blog.opencounseling.com/
  location_search

Bosnia & Herzegovina: Suicide
Hotline 080 05 03 05

Botswana

- Emergency 911

- Suicide Hotline
  +2673911270

- More Hotlines: blog.
  opencounseling.com/
  hotlines-bw

- In-Person Counseling:
  blog.opencounseling.com/
  location_search

Brazil

- Emergency 188

- More Hotlines: blog.
  opencounseling.com/
  hotlines-br

- In-Person Counseling:
  blog.opencounseling.com/
  location_search

Bulgaria

- Emergency 112

- Suicide Hotline 0035
  9249 17 223

Burundi

- Emergency 117

- More Hotlines: blog.
  opencounseling.com/
  hotlines-bi

- In-Person Counseling:
  blog.opencounseling.com/
  location_search

Burkina Faso

- Emergency 17

- More Hotlines: blog.
  opencounseling.com/
  hotlines-bf

- In-Person Counseling: blog.opencounseling.com/location_search

Canada

- Emergency 911
- Suicide Hotline 1 (833) 456 4566
- More Hotlines: blog. opencounseling.com/hotlines-ca
- In-Person Counseling: blog.opencounseling.com/location_search

Chad

- Emergency 2251-1237
- More Hotlines: blog. opencounseling.com/hotlines-td
- In-Person Counseling: blog.opencounseling.com/location_search

China

- Emergency 110
- Suicide Hotline 800-810-1117

Colombia

- 24/7 Helpline in Barranquilla 1(00 57 5) 372 27 27
- 24/7 Hotline Bogota (57-1) 323 24 25
- More Hotlines: blog. opencounseling.com/hotlines-co
- In-Person Counseling: blog.opencounseling.com/location_search

Congo: Emergency 117

Costa Rica

- Emergency 911
- Suicide Hotline 506-253-5439
- More Hotlines: blog. opencounseling.com/hotlines-cr
- In-Person Counseling: blog.opencounseling.com/location_search

Croatia

- Emergency 112
- More Hotlines: blog. opencounseling.com/hotlines-hr

Cyprus:

- Emergency 112
- Suicide Hotline 8000 7773

Czech Republic: Emergency 112

Denmark

- Emergency 112
- Suicide Hotline 4570201201

Dominican Republic

- Emergency 911
- Suicide Hotline (809) 562-3500
- More Hotlines: blog. opencounseling.com/ hotlines-do
- In-Person Counseling: blog.opencounseling.com/ location_search

Ecuador

- Emergency 911
- More Hotlines: blog. opencounseling.com/ hotlines-ec
- In-Person Counseling: blog.opencounseling.com/ location_search

Egypt

- Emergency 122
- Suicide Hotline 131114
- More Hotlines: blog. opencounseling.com/ hotlines-eg
- In-Person Counseling: blog.opencounseling.com/ location_search

El Salvador

- Emergency 911
- Suicide Hotline 126
- More Hotlines: blog. opencounseling.com/ hotlines-sv
- In-Person Counseling: blog.opencounseling.com/ location_search

Equatorial Guinea

- Emergency 114
- More Hotlines: blog. opencounseling.com/ hotlines-gq
- In-Person Counseling: blog.opencounseling.com/ location_search

Estonia

- Emergency 112
- Suicide Hotline 3726558088
- In Russian 3726555688

Ethiopia

- Emergency 911
- More Hotlines: blog. opencounseling.com/ hotlines-et
- In-Person Counseling: blog.opencounseling.com/ location_search

Finland

- Emergency 112
- Suicide Hotline 010 195 202

France

- Emergency 112
- Suicide Hotline 0145394000
- More Hotlines: blog. opencounseling.com/ hotlines-fr

Germany

- Emergency 112
- Suicide Hotline 0800 111 0 111
- More Hotlines: blog. opencounseling.com/ hotlines-de

Ghana

- Emergency 999
- Suicide Hotline 2332 444 71279
- More Hotlines: blog. opencounseling.com/ hotlines-gh
- In-Person Counseling: blog.opencounseling.com/ location_search

Greece: Emergency 1018

Guatemala

- Emergency 110
- Suicide Hotline 5392-5953
- More Hotlines: blog. opencounseling.com/ hotlines-gt
- In-Person Counseling: blog.opencounseling.com/ location_search

Guinea

- Emergency 117
- More Hotlines: blog. opencounseling.com/ hotlines-gn
- In-Person Counseling: blog.opencounseling.com/ location_search

Guinea Bissau

- Emergency 117
- More Hotlines: blog. opencounseling.com/ hotlines-gw
- In-Person Counseling: blog.opencounseling.com/ location_search

Guyana

- Emergency 999
- Suicide Hotline 223-0001

Holland: Suicide
Hotline 09000767

Hong Kong

- Emergency 999
- Suicide Hotline 852 2382 0000

Hungary

- Emergency 112
- Suicide Hotline 116123

India

- Emergency 112
- Suicide Hotline 8888817666
- More Hotlines: blog. opencounseling.com/ hotlines-in
- In-Person Counseling: blog.opencounseling.com/ location_search

Indonesia

- Emergency 112
- Suicide Hotline 1-800-273-8255
- More Hotlines: blog. opencounseling.com/ hotlines-id

Iran

- Emergency 110
- Suicide Hotline 1480

Ireland

- Emergency 116123
- Suicide Hotline +4408457909090

- More Hotlines: blog.
  opencounseling.com/
  hotlines-ie

- In-Person Counseling:
  blog.opencounseling.com/
  location_search

Israel

- Emergency 100

- Suicide Hotline 1201

- More Hotlines: blog.
  opencounseling.com/
  hotlines-il

Italy

- Emergency 112

- Suicide
  Hotline 800860022

Jamaica: Suicide Hotline 1-888-429-KARE (5273)

Japan

- Emergency 110

- Suicide
  Hotline 810352869090

Jordan

- Emergency 911

- Suicide Hotline 110

- More Hotlines: blog.
  opencounseling.com/
  hotlines-jo

- In-Person Counseling:
  blog.opencounseling.com/
  location_search

Kenya

- Emergency 999

- Suicide
  Hotline 722178177

- More Hotlines: blog.
  opencounseling.com/
  hotlines-ke

- In-Person Counseling:
  blog.opencounseling.com/
  location_search

Kuwait

- Emergency 112

- Suicide Hotline 94069304

- More Hotlines: blog.
  opencounseling.com/
  hotlines-kw

- In-Person Counseling:
  blog.opencounseling.com/
  location_search

Latvia

- Emergency 113

- Suicide Hotline
  371 67222922

Lebanon: Suicide Hotline 1564

Liberia

- Emergency 911
- Suicide Hotline 6534308
- More Hotlines: blog. opencounseling.com/ hotlines-lr
- In-Person Counseling: blog.opencounseling.com/ location_search

Lithuania

- Emergency 112
- Suicide Hotline 8 800 28888
- More Hotlines: tuesi.lt

Luxembourg

- Emergency 112
- Suicide Hotline 352 45 45 45

Madagascar

- Emergency 117
- More Hotlines: blog. opencounseling.com/ hotlines-mg
- In-Person Counseling: blog.opencounseling.com/ location_search

Malaysia

- Emergency 999
- Suicide Hotline (06) 2842500
- More Hotlines: blog. opencounseling.com/ hotlines-my

Mali

- Emergency 8000-1115
- More Hotlines: blog. opencounseling.com/ hotlines-ml
- In-Person Counseling: blog.opencounseling.com/ location_search

Malta: Suicide Hotline 179

Mauritius

- Emergency 112
- Suicide Hotline +230 800 93 93

Mexico

- Emergency 911
- Suicide Hotline 5255102550
- More Hotlines: blog. opencounseling.com/ hotlines-mx

- In-Person Counseling: blog.opencounseling.com/location_search

Netherlands

- Emergency 112
- Suicide Hotline 900 0113
- More Hotlines: blog.opencounseling.com/hotlines-nl

New Zealand

- Emergency 111
- Suicide Hotline 1737
- More Hotlines: blog.opencounseling.com/hotlines-nz
- In-Person Counseling: blog.opencounseling.com/location_search

Niger

- Emergency 112
- More Hotlines: blog.opencounseling.com/hotlines-ne
- In-Person Counseling: blog.opencounseling.com/location_search

Nigeria

- Suicide Hotline 234 8092106493
- More Hotlines: blog.opencounseling.com/hotlines-ng
- In-Person Counseling: blog.opencounseling.com/location_search

Norway

- Emergency 112
- Suicide Hotline +4781533300

Pakistan

- Emergency 115
- More Hotlines: blog.opencounseling.com/hotlines-pk
- In-Person Counseling: blog.opencounseling.com/location_search

Peru

- Emergency 911
- Suicide Hotline 381-3695
- More Hotlines: blog.opencounseling.com/hotlines-pe
- In-Person Counseling: blog.opencounseling.com/location_search

Philippines

- Emergency 911

- Suicide Hotline 028969191

- More Hotlines: blog. opencounseling.com/ hotlines-ph

- In-Person Counseling: blog.opencounseling.com/ location_search

Poland

- Emergency 112

- Suicide Hotline 5270000

Portugal

- Emergency 112

- Suicide Hotline 21 854 07 40 and 8 96 898 21 50

Qatar

- Emergency 999

- More Hotlines: blog. opencounseling.com/ hotlines-qa

- In-Person Counseling: blog.opencounseling.com/ location_search

Romania

- Emergency 112

- Suicide Hotline 0800 801200

- More Hotlines: blog. opencounseling.com/ hotlines-ro

Russia

- Emergency 112

- Suicide Hotline 0078202577577

Saint Vincent and the Grenadines: Suicide Hotline 9784 456 1044

São Tomé and Príncipe

- Suicide Hotline (239) 222-12-22 ext. 123

- More Hotlines: blog. opencounseling.com/ hotlines-st

- In-Person Counseling: blog.opencounseling.com/ location_search

Saudi Arabia

- Emergency 112

- More Hotlines: blog. opencounseling.com/ hotlines-sa

- In-Person Counseling: blog.opencounseling.com/ location_search

Serbia: Suicide Hotline (+381) 21-6623-393

Senegal

- Emergency 17
- More Hotlines: blog. opencounseling.com/ hotlines-sn
- In-Person Counseling: blog.opencounseling.com/ location_search

Singapore

- Emergency 999
- Suicide Hotline 1 800 2214444
- More Hotlines: blog. opencounseling.com/ hotlines-sg

Spain

- Emergency 112
- Suicide Hotline 914590050
- More Hotlines: blog. opencounseling.com/ hotlines-es

South Africa

- Emergency 10111
- Suicide Hotline 0514445691

- More Hotlines: blog. opencounseling.com/ hotlines-za
- In-Person Counseling: blog.opencounseling.com/ location_search

South Korea

- Emergency 112
- Suicide Hotline (02) 7158600
- More Hotlines: blog. opencounseling.com/ hotlines-kr

Sri Lanka: Suicide Hotline 011 057 2222662

Sudan

- Suicide Hotline (249) 11-555-253
- More Hotlines: blog. opencounseling.com/ hotlines-sd
- In-Person Counseling: blog.opencounseling.com/ location_search

Sweden

- Emergency 112
- Suicide Hotline 46317112400

- More Hotlines: blog. opencounseling.com/ hotlines-se

Switzerland

- Emergency 112

- Suicide Hotline 143

- More Hotlines: blog. opencounseling.com/ hotlines-ch

Tanzania

- Emergency 112

- More Hotlines: blog. opencounseling.com/ hotlines-tz

- In-Person Counseling: blog.opencounseling.com/ location_search

Thailand: Suicide Hotline (02) 713-6793

Tonga: Suicide Hotline 23000

Trinidad and Tobago: Suicide Hotline (868) 645 2800

Tunisia

- Emergency 197

- More Hotlines: blog. opencounseling.com/ hotlines-tn

- In-Person Counseling: blog.opencounseling.com/ location_search

Turkey: Emergency 112

Uganda

- Emergency 112

- Suicide Hotline 0800 21 21 21

- More Hotlines: blog. opencounseling.com/ hotlines-ug

- In-Person Counseling: blog.opencounseling.com/ location_search

United Arab Emirates

- Suicide Hotline 800 46342

- More Hotlines: blog. opencounseling.com/ hotlines-ae

- In-Person Counseling: blog.opencounseling.com/ location_search

United Kingdom

- Emergency 112

- Suicide Hotline 0800 689 5652

- More Hotlines: blog. opencounseling.com/ hotlines-gb

- In-Person Counseling: blog.opencounseling.com/location_search

United States

- Emergency 911
- Suicide Hotline 988
- More Hotlines: blog.opencounseling.com/hotlines-us
- In-Person Counseling: blog.opencounseling.com/location_search

Zambia

- Emergency 999
- Suicide Hotline +260960264040
- More Hotlines: blog.opencounseling.com/hotlines-zm
- In-Person Counseling: blog.opencounseling.com/location_search

Zimbabwe

- Emergency 999
- Suicide Hotline 080 12 333 333
- More Hotlines: blog.opencounseling.com/hotlines-zw

- In-Person Counseling: blog.opencounseling.com/location_search

Suicidal? In danger? Need help? This is a list of suicide hotlines worldwide.

- blog.opencounseling.com/suicide-hotlines

Emergency numbers worldwide can be found on these sites:

- www.psychologytoday.com/us/basics/suicide/suicide-prevention-hotlines-resources-worldwide
- blog.opencounseling.com/suicide-hotlines
- www.suicidestop.com/call_a_hotline.html

Safety Plan Template

There are no "wrong" answers. If you can, have someone help you with this. Share this plan with the people you identify in the last question below. Have this plan somewhere people can find it if there is a crisis—maybe a wallet—or have someone you trust keep a copy in case of emergencies who will keep it confidential for you.

What are my warning signs? What are my thoughts, actions, and feelings I have when I start to think suicidal thoughts?

What physical feelings do I have (racing heart, pain, shortness of breath, twitching, etc.)?

What emotions or states do I feel (sadness, overwhelm, aloneness, grief, shame, release, fear, etc.)?

What thoughts do I have when I begin to feel suicidal thoughts emerging (thoughts of hurting myself or engaging in picking at my fingernails or self-mutilation, thoughts that everyone hates me, that I am unloved, that no one cares, that others would be better off without me, etc.)?

What will let me know when I need to activate my safety plan? What warning signs will there be?

How will I execute this plan? Will I call an emergency contact or supporter first, go to the emergency room, or call a caregiver or wellness professional? Call my therapist? What is the order of my plan, and my strategy?

What do I do to cope with these feelings when they come? How do I cope with other things that happen during the day? Do any of these coping mechanisms work for me, and can I use a technique that will help me? If so, what is that (meditation, breathing, taking a pause, self-care, exercise, creative practice of some kind, etc.)?

What can I do by myself to keep myself safe?

What people, places, and activities can help me forget these thoughts? What distractions can I use?

What things around me can I remove to help me feel safer? These things might include guns, knives, firearms, medications, cars, overly stressful situations, toxic people, toxic spaces, and anything that's tempting when you are in a suicidal thought pattern or that pushes you into a space of feeling desperate.

Who is in my support system, and how do I contact them? This will include family, friends, therapists, doctors, healers, teachers, mentors, etc. Write down their names and contact info clearly, so that someone who is helping you can read them. Divide them up into the following:

Emergency Contact Information

- Doctors and caregivers

- Therapists

- Healers

- Supporters

- People who can take you to the hospital or treatment if you need it

- People who can check in on you if you need it

AFTERWORD

I am sincerely grateful to all of you, and I hope you got something out of this book. I would love to connect with you, either through my Meetups, groups, podcasts, or social media. If you see me standing in line for coffee somewhere, please introduce yourself. I'd love to meet you!

Please share your stories with us. Keep sharing your stories until they are seen by those of us who need to see them. They matter. You matter.

If this book was helpful to you, please leave a positive review where applicable. It will help other folks who need support to find it.

If you would like to be on my mailing list or inquire about working together, please go to www.julianajbruno.com.

If you would like to listen to my podcast, please listen on any of the platforms listed here: linktr.ee/i.care.about.you.podcast.

If you would like to be part of the social refugee project, go here and inquire: www.socialrefugees.org.

If you would like to connect with my Meetups and see where else you can keep in touch with my organization, click here: linktr.ee/socialrefugees.

REFERENCE NOTES/INDEX/
READING LIST

Please see the guide to some of the national organizations working on suicide awareness and prevention.

Books:

- *The 5 Love Languages: The Secret to Love that Lasts*, by Dr. Gary Chapman

- *Signs: The Secret Language of the Universe,* by Laura Lynn Jackson

- *The Smell of Rain on Dust,* by Martín Prechtel

- *It's OK That You're Not OK,* by Megan Devine

- *The Myth of Normal,* by Gabor Maté MD, Daniel Maté

- *The Creative Act*, by Rick Rubin

- *Untamed,* by Glennon Doyle

- *Buy Yourself the F*cking Lilies,* by Tara Schuster

- *What Happened to You?* by Oprah Winfrey, Bruce D. Perry

- *Strong,* by Eric Rosswood (Children, YA)

- *The Woman's Book of Strength: Meditation for Wisdom, Balance & Power*, by Sue Patton Thoele

- *Let Go Now: Embracing Detachment,* by Karen Casey

- *Mindfulness for Warriors,* by Kim Colegrove

- *Parenting the New Teen in the Age of Anxiety: A Complete Guide to Your Child's Stressed, Depressed, Expanded, Amazing Adolescence,* by Dr. John Duffy

- *The Velveteen Rabbit,* by Margery Williams

Movie Reference:

- *Nightmare Before Christmas,* Tim Burton

Articles:

- www.healthline.com/health/mental-health/types-of-meditation#mantra-meditation

- www.everydayhealth.com/alternative-health/living-with/ways-practice-breath-focused-meditation

- ctsciencecenter.org/blog/the-science-of-stress-understanding-your-stress-response

- www.powerofpositivity.com/habits-become-authentic-self

- www.psychologytoday.com/us/blog/feeling-it/201409/18-science-backed-reasons-try-loving-kindness-meditation

- www.psychologytoday.com/us/basics/therapy/therapy-types-and-modalities

- www.mindbodygreen.com/articles/types-of-therapy

- positivepsychology.com/somatic-experiencing/#Somatic%20Experiencing%20Explained

- www.psychologytoday.com/us/blog/sapient-nature/201401/the-need-love

IN DEEPEST GRATITUDE

Thank you to Brenda Knight, my publisher, who helped me see the vision for this book. Thank you to everyone at Mango Publishing who patiently and enthusiastically supported this project. Thank you to Jenny Knott, who helped me to craft my book proposal into something understandable. I deeply thank Bonnie Eslinger, friend and organizer, for graciously offering her home as a gathering place for our writing group on Saturday mornings. To my gifted fellow writers in the group, who inspired me with their talent and grace. To Thuy Nguyen, my sincerest thank you for your ability to listen deeply and for guiding me to my inner medicine. To all the wonderful healers, writers, and therapists who wrote in support of this project. Thank you to my team of dreamers. Thank you to my sisters, Tina Smalldon and Darlene Busi, for always being there. I love you dearly. To my BFF Domenic, who is always there to celebrate a milestone in my life. To my daughters and co-dreamers, Phoenix and Avalon, who never cease to inspire me. You are my gurus and teachers in this life and without you I would have surely missed out on much of the beauty this life has to offer. To Brennan for his support and input around the meaning of life, death, and Midwestern perspectives. To all my podcast subscribers and listeners. To everyone who supported me through this project. Special thank you to all the people who have supported me through the twists and turns of life. Support is the greatest gift you can give another, and I appreciate you all every day. To those of you who have come to this book for whatever reason: thank you. Know that you are not alone. You are loved. You have value. You have worth.

ABOUT THE AUTHOR

Juliana J. Bruno, a.k.a. Juliana Jay (she, they) is a transformational coach and meditation teacher. They are the host and creator of the *I Care About You Podcast* and founder of the grassroots suicide awareness group socialrefugees.org. Juliana facilitates healing circles and groups, both in person and online.

Juliana is a graduate of UC Santa Cruz, where they received a degree in Molecular, Cellular, and Developmental Biology. They studied meditation and mindfulness under the instruction of some of the most prominent teachers of our time, including Jack Kornfield and Tara Brach. They are also an award-winning artist and photographer and have worked as a manager and director for universities and schools and, most recently, as Executive Director (interim) of Ace Makerspace in Oakland, CA.

They live in the Bay Area of California and enjoy surfing, yoga, walks with their dog, Sweet Jane, and creating functional art installations.

Mango Publishing, established in 2014, publishes an eclectic list of books by diverse authors—both new and established voices—on topics ranging from business, personal growth, women's empowerment, LGBTQ studies, health, and spirituality to history, popular culture, time management, decluttering, lifestyle, mental wellness, aging, and sustainable living. We were named 2019 *and* 2020's #1 fastest growing independent publisher by *Publishers Weekly*. Our success is driven by our main goal, which is to publish high-quality books that will entertain readers as well as make a positive difference in their lives.

Our readers are our most important resource; we value your input, suggestions, and ideas. We'd love to hear from you—after all, we are publishing books for you!

Please stay in touch with us and follow us at:

Facebook: Mango Publishing
Twitter: @MangoPublishing
Instagram: @MangoPublishing
LinkedIn: Mango Publishing
Pinterest: Mango Publishing
Newsletter: mangopublishinggroup.com/newsletter

Join us on Mango's journey to reinvent publishing, one book at a time.

Printed in the USA
CPSIA information can be obtained
at www.ICGtesting.com
JSHW030250090824
67865JS00003B/6